Within Prison Walls

Thomas Mott Osborne

Within Prison Walls

ISBN: 978-1-64799-978-0

CONTENTS

CONTENTS

CHAPTER I
WHY I WENT TO PRISON

Many years back, in my early boyhood, I was taken through Auburn Prison. It has always been the main object of interest in our town, and I was a small sized unit in a party of sightseers. No incident of childhood made a more vivid impression upon me. The dark, scowling faces bent over their tasks; the hideous striped clothing, which carried with it an unexplainable sense of shame; the ugly close cropped heads and shaven faces; the horrible sinuous lines of outcast humanity crawling along in the dreadful lockstep; the whole thing aroused such terror in my imagination that I never recovered from the painful impression. All the nightmares and evil dreams of my childhood centered about the figure of an escaped convict. He chased me along dark streets, where I was unable to run fast or cry aloud; he peeked through windows at me as I lay in bed, even after the shades had been pinned close to escape his evil eye; as I ascended a flight of stairs in dreamland and looked back, he would come creeping through an open door, holding a long knife in his hand, while my mother all unconscious of danger sat reading under the shaded library lamp; he was a visitor frequent enough to make night hideous for a time, and it was many long years before he took a departure which I trust is final.

After this early experience I carefully avoided the Prison. Its gray stone walls frowned from across the street every time I departed or arrived on a New York Central train, but I made no effort to go again inside. In fact I persistently refused to join my friends whenever they made a visit there; once had been quite enough.

So it was not until many years afterward that I again passed within prison walls. Then my official connection with the Junior Republic and its successful training of wild and mischievous boys brought me in touch with the Prison System. I had been interested in the Elmira Reformatory and had visited Mr. Brockway, the superintendent of that institution. I became acquainted, quite by chance, with a certain prisoner in Sing Sing, and through him interested in other prisoners, there and in Auburn. In due time, I began to appreciate the importance of the general Prison Problem

1

and the difficulties of its solution. Also I felt that my experience in the Junior Republic had given me a possible clew to that solution.

Thus I was drawn to the prison almost in spite of myself; and, becoming more and more interested, I felt that there was great need of some one's making a study at first hand—some one sympathetic but not sentimental—of the thoughts and habits of the men whom the state holds in confinement. It is easy to read a textbook on civil government and then fancy we know exactly how the administration of a state is conducted; but the actual facts of practical politics are often miles asunder from the textbook theory. In the same way "the Criminal" has been extensively studied, and deductions as to his instincts, habits and character drawn from the measurements of his ears and nose; but I wanted to get acquainted with the man himself, the man behind the statistics.

So the idea of some day entering prison and actually living the life of a convict first occurred to me more than three years ago. Talking with a friend, after his release from prison, concerning his own experience and the need of changes in the System, I brought forward the idea that it was impossible for those of us on the outside to deal in full sympathy and understanding with the man within the walls until we had come in close personal contact with him, and had had something like a physical experience of similar conditions. We discussed how the thing could be done in case the circumstances ever came about so that it would become desirable for me to do it. He agreed as to the general proposition; but nevertheless shook his head somewhat doubtfully. "There is no question but that you'd learn a lot," he said; then added, "but I think you'd find it rather a tough experience." He made the suggestion that if ever the plan were carried out autumn would be the best season, as the cells would be least uncomfortable at that time of year.

Time passed, and while I continued to have an interest in the Prison Problem, the interest was a passive rather than an active one. Then on a red-letter day in the summer of 1912, being confined to the house by a slight illness, I read Donald Lowrie's book, "My Life in Prison." That vivid picture of prison conditions, written so simply yet with such power and such complete and evident sincerity, stirred me to the depths. It made me feel that I had no right any longer to be silent or indifferent; I must do my share to remove the foulest blot upon our social system.

Thereafter when called upon to speak in public, I usually made Prison Reform the subject of my talk, advancing certain ideas gathered from my experience with the boys of the Junior Republic, endeavoring not only to crystalize my own views as to the

2

prisons but to get others to turn their thoughts in the same direction.

Finally came an appointment by Governor Sulzer to a State Commission on Prison Reform, suggested to the Governor by Judge Riley, the new Superintendent of Prisons. My position as chairman of the Commission made it seem desirable, if not necessary, to inform myself to the utmost as to the inner conditions of the prisons and the needs of the inmates. I do not mean that it was necessary to reinvestigate the material aspect of the prisons—it is known already that the conditions at Sing Sing are barbaric, and those at Auburn medieval—but that it was desirable to get all possible light regarding the actual effect of the System as a whole, or specific parts of it, upon the prisoners.

I began to feel, therefore, that the time had come to carry out the plan which had been so long in the background of my mind. I discussed it long and earnestly with a certain dear friend, who gave me needed encouragement; the Superintendent of Prisons and the Warden at Auburn approved; and, last but not least, an intelligent convict in whom I confided thought it a decidedly good idea. None of us, to be sure, realized the way in which the thing was actually to work out. It became a much more vital and far-reaching experiment than we had any of us expected or could have dared to hope. We were not prepared for the way in which the imaginations of many people, both in and out of prison, were to be touched and stimulated.

Originally I had intended to enter the prison in disguise. In that way I thought one could learn the most, as one would stand a much better chance of seeing the System in its normal working order. Upon mature reflection, however, this idea was given up. The Warden felt strongly that there would be danger of the best possible disguise being penetrated where so many pairs of sharp eyes were on the watch; and I agreed with him that in such event I could not avoid being set down as a spy by both officers and prisoners, and my real object fatally misunderstood. The little additional knowledge I might secure by being unknown would not pay for the danger of complete failure. In this conclusion the intelligent convict joined, for he had pointed out from the first that, while there were certain obvious disadvantages in being known, yet there were also certain advantages great enough to more than counterbalance. He said that if I could spare two months for the visit it would be better to come disguised, but that it would certainly take as long as that to get into the game. "You know we're awful suspicious," he added, by way of explanation; "and we don't open up to any new fellow until we know he's on the level." He maintained therefore that, having only a week, I had much better make no secret of it, but come in my own person. His view was confirmed by the event. I not only learned far more than if I had been unknown, but I so gained the confidence of the prisoners that many of them have become my devoted and valued friends.

The account in the following chapters of my week in Auburn Prison is taken from the pages of a journal I kept during my confinement. In that I jotted down, day by day, every incident no matter how trivial it seemed at the time; so that I possess a very complete record of my week in prison.

As I have transcribed the pages of the diary I have lived over again every moment of that remarkably vivid experience, finding that almost every act, every word, every detail, is fairly burned into my memory. I have scarcely needed the pages of the journal, nor the long account of our week together which my working partner in the basket shop, Jack Murphy, wrote out at my request.

I shall not attempt to draw up any bill of indictment against the Prison System, or to suggest specific improvements, either in general principles or administrative details; I shall simply set down the facts and my feelings as accurately as I can.

One final word by way of introduction. Many newspapers, presumably reflecting the impressions of a considerable number of individuals, have expressed the idea that nothing of value could possibly have been obtained because I was not a real convict; although the same newspapers would probably be the first to discredit any statements a real convict might make. Foreseeing such criticism, I had tried to forestall it in the remarks I addressed to the prisoners the day before my experiment began; and if some of my editorial critics had taken the trouble to read their own press dispatches, they might have been saved some distress of mind. No one could have understood better than I did at the outset, that it is impossible to place yourself exactly in the shoes of a man who has been sentenced to prison for an actual crime; I did not expect to do so. No one, so far as I know, has ever yet succeeded in putting himself precisely in the place of another in any given set of circumstances; yet that does not keep us from constantly studying and analyzing the human problem. It still remains true that "The proper study of mankind is man." In this particular instance, perhaps some things of value were obtained for the very reason that I was not a criminal. Possibly I could judge of some matters with a juster appreciation than could any man suffering involuntary imprisonment. It did, in fact, surprise me very much that anyone

4

could succeed to so great an extent in putting himself in the place and in sharing so many of the sensations of an actual prisoner. Time and again I heard from others the expression of thoughts and feelings which I recognized as those which had swept over me; and I found that, partly by force of imagination and environment and partly by the actual physical conditions of confinement, one could really come into astonishingly close sympathy and understanding with the prisoner. The truth of this can, I believe, be seen in my narrative and has been demonstrated many times since my release.

Of course all this would not have been possible had not the attitude of both officers and inmates been just what it was. As I look back, it seems to me that all hands played their parts to perfection. The strict orders of the Warden that I was to receive no favors whatever and must be treated exactly like any ordinary inmate, were literally carried out—except in the two or three unimportant instances noted in my journal. But far more remarkable was the attitude of the prisoners. An outsider would never have detected a look or an action to indicate that there was any difference between "Tom Brown" and any other inmate of the institution. Of course it could not be absolutely the same; it was not possible for me to escape being an object of interest; and I often felt around me a sort of suppressed excitement; although, as I glanced again at the stolid gray automatons, among whom I marched or sat at mess, I would think it must be only my imagination—a reflex of my own excitement. Still I would catch an occasional smile, a wink, a lifting of an eyebrow, the ghost of a nod—to show that those silent figures were not really indifferent to my presence among them. And as I went to my cell for the night, there might be a momentary pause by a gray-clothed figure at the door, and a low whisper, "How does it go, Tom?" All such things, however, might well have been in the case of any new convict who had figured in the public prints and had thus become an object of common interest.

After all possible deductions have been made, the fact remains that my experiment met conditions at the prison which, thanks to officers and inmates, led to a large measure of gratifying success. It is hard to see how, from any point of view, the experience could have been improved upon; it is hard to see how I could possibly have learned more in a week than I did. If it were to be done over again, there is nothing whatever that I would change. It has been not only a novel and most interesting experience, it has been a wonderful revelation. I have come out of prison with a new conception of the inherent nobility of human nature, a new belief in the power of men to respond to the right conditions and the right

5

appeal. I have come out with a new sense of human brotherhood, a new faith in God.

CHAPTER II
SUNDAY'S JOURNAL

September 28, 1913. 9.30 P. M.

All is ready for my great adventure. Indeed the first steps have been taken. This morning I went down to the Prison to speak at the chapel exercises as planned; but arrived early, about nine o'clock, at Warden Rattigan's request, in order to inform the Chaplain as to what I am proposing to do. He seemed very much surprised and pleased. The Warden also explained the matter to the Principal Keeper; but I shall not attempt to venture a guess at his feelings, for I was not present. I can imagine, however, that the official view may not be one altogether in sympathy with my experiment. The official mind, as a rule, prefers to have things viewed strictly from the "congregation side"; it does not approve of interlopers behind the scenes; which is not, perhaps, altogether unnatural.

When the prisoners are all assembled, the Chaplain leads the way and we walk down the aisle of the chapel or assembly room—the latter name seems more appropriate, as there is very little there to suggest religion. Ascending the platform, we are greeted by a cordial round of applause; the men have apparently not forgotten my talk to them in the yard last July, when I explained what our Prison Reform Commission hopes to accomplish, and asked their assistance.

I take my seat upon the platform and, while awaiting my turn to speak, endeavor to listen to the service. Before me sit rows and rows of men in gray trousers and faded shirts, upward of 1,300—not a full house, for a considerable number are out in the road-building camps. Gray predominates—not only in the gray clothes but in the heads and faces. There are a few bright spots of youth and manly vigor, and some black negro heads, but the general impression is gray; gray, and faded, and prematurely old. It is a sad audience, to which a sinister aspect is given by the sight of the guards—silent, alert, blue-clothed figures, youthful for the most part, seated with watchful eyes and weapons handy, each in a raised chair near his own particular company.

But, although a sad audience to look upon, it is, as I have found on previous occasions, a most wonderfully sensitive and responsive audience to address. Each point of the discourse is caught with extraordinary quickness; every slight attempt at humor is seized upon with pathetic avidity. The speaker soon finds himself stimulated and carried along, as by a strange and powerful force he has never felt before. It is an exciting and exhilarating experience to talk to a prison audience; but one must take good care not to be a bore, nor to try any cheap oratorical tricks; for it is not only a keen and critical audience, it is a merciless one.

This morning I am not at all afraid of boring the hearers; but I do wonder whether they will fully take in my meaning; and how those who do understand will like the idea of my coming among them; and if some of them understand and sympathize, will it be a few only, or a majority; and if a majority, how large; and will the minority resent it sufficiently to be disagreeable?

These are some of the questions which go buzzing through my mind as I sit trying in vain to listen to the singing of the prison choir and the Scripture lesson which the Chaplain is reading. Finally I am called upon to speak; and as I advance to the front of the stage another round of applause comes from the audience. It has rather a startling effect upon one, for applause in the prison chapel has always somewhat the character of an explosion—an explosion of pent-up feelings denied any ordinary freedom of expression. Hand-clapping is the only form permitted, and it sounds like the snapping of firecrackers.

I advance to the front of the stage and stumble through the first words of explanation as to the reasons for having my speech carefully written out—in order to avoid any possible misunderstanding afterward as to what I really have said. Then I clear my throat and read the address which follows.

> The Superintendent of Prisons and Warden Rattigan have kindly given me permission to carry out a plan which has been in my mind for some time; and to carry it out successfully I need your coöperation—both officials and prisoners.
>
> As most of you doubtless know, I am chairman of the Commission on Prison Reform appointed by Governor Sulzer to examine into the Prison System of New York State, determine what changes would be desirable and formulate

7

legislation necessary to bring about such changes. The members of the Commission since their appointment have been quietly at work informing themselves as to the manner in which the present System works out, its effect upon prisoners, the measure of its success as a means of reducing crime throughout the state.

It must be evident that any such examination, seriously undertaken, is an extremely complex and difficult matter. Not only are trustworthy statistics absolutely lacking by which to determine the more obvious facts, but statistics are manifestly impossible to secure regarding the deepest and most important parts of the problem—for instance, as to the psychological effect on the prisoners themselves of the Prison System, both as a whole and as to certain specific rules and regulations.

For much of the most important work of the Commission, therefore, we must fall back on such experience of life and knowledge of human nature as its members may possess. And it is with a desire to extend my own knowledge and experience in the service of the Commission that I ask your help in carrying out the plan to which I have referred.

When a man wishes to understand as fully as possible the temper and character of the people of a foreign country—England or France, Germany, India, China—he can consult a great deal of printed matter; but he will not be satisfied until he has made a personal visit to the country itself. For instance, I have but the merest smattering of the French language, and I have been privileged to know socially but very few Frenchmen, yet my visits to France have given me an infinitely better idea of the country and people than I could ever have received from books. The actual sights and sounds of a country seem to provide the foundation for a far better understanding of its history, a more thorough appreciation of all that can be read and heard of it thereafter.

If this sympathy and understanding, coming from a vivid personal experience, is desirable in the case of a foreign country, it is even more necessary in the case of a group of men set apart by society, such as this community of the prison; for in your case the conditions under which you live are more unnatural and less easy for most people to grasp than those of a foreign country. Moreover, most of the books that have been written about you by so-called penologists and other "experts" are written, so far as I can determine, from such an outside standpoint and with so little

8

intelligent sympathy and vital understanding that I am inclined to the belief that very few of them are of any particular value. Indeed many are positively harmful; for they are based upon the false and cruel assumption that the prisoner is not a human being like the rest of us, but a strange sort of animal called a "criminal"—wholly different in his instincts, feelings and actions from the rest of mankind.

I am curious to find out, therefore, whether I am right; whether our Prison System is as unintelligent as I think it is; whether it flies in the face of all common sense and all human nature, as I think it does; whether, guided by sympathy and experience, we cannot find something far better to take its place, as I believe we can.

So by permission of the authorities and with your help, I am coming here to learn what I can at first hand. I have put myself on trial in the court of conscience and a verdict has been rendered of "guilty"—guilty of having lived for many years of my life indifferent to and ignorant of what was going on behind these walls. For this crime I have sentenced myself to a short term at hard labor in Auburn Prison (with commutation, of course, for good behavior). I expect to begin serving my sentence this week. I am coming here to live your life; to be housed, clothed, fed, treated in all respects like one of you. I want to see for myself exactly what your life is like, not as viewed from the outside looking in, but from the inside looking out.

Of course I am not so foolish as to think that I can see it from exactly your point of view. Manifestly a man cannot be a real prisoner when he may at any moment let down the bars and walk out; and spending a few hours or days in a cell is quite a different thing from a weary round of weeks, months, years. Nor is prison a mere matter of clothes, they cannot make a convict any more than they can make a gentleman. I realize perfectly that my point of view cannot be yours; but neither when I go to Paris is my point of view that of a Frenchman. Just as an American may perhaps understand some things about Paris which are not so clear to the average Frenchman, so perhaps a short residence among you here may enable me to judge some things about the Prison System more accurately than those who live too close to the problem to see it in its true perspective.

A word to the officials. My plan will not altogether succeed unless I am treated exactly like these other men. I ask you, therefore, to aid me by making no discrimination in my favor. Relax your regular discipline not a jot because I am here. Give

9

me the same guidance as these others—but no more. If I offend against the rules, deal out to me the same punishment—I shall expect it.

Here again I do not deceive myself; I realize perfectly that I shall not see the Prison System in quite its normal running order. Things can hardly, with the best intentions, keep going exactly the same while I am here. Long ago when I was a very young school commissioner I found out that neither teachers nor scholars can behave quite naturally when a member of the school board is present. But let me assure you that I come not on any errand of official investigation. I come in no sense as a spy upon officers or inmates; I come not to discover anything; I come solely to test, so far as I can, the effect of the system upon the mind of the prisoner. I shall study myself, rather than you; or rather, I shall study you through myself.

Perhaps many of you will think, as many outside the walls will think, that at best this action is quixotic—another "fool's errand, by one of the fools." I shall not argue the matter further. I believe that I fully realize the shortcomings which will attend the experience, yet still I shall undertake it. For somehow, deep down, I have the feeling that after I have really lived among you, marched in your lines, shared your food, gone to the same cells at night, and in the morning looked out at the pieces of God's sunlight through the same iron bars—that then, and not until then, can I feel the knowledge which will break down the barriers between my soul and the souls of my brothers.

A final word to you all. When I come among you do your best to forget who I am. Think of me only as a new and quite uninteresting arrival. Think of me not as a member of the Prison Reform Commission, nor as the fellow townsman of you officers, but as plain Tom Brown or Jones or Robinson, sent by the courts for some breach of the law and who is no more to you for the present than any other Tom, Dick or Harry. Some day in the future, after I have done my time, perhaps my experience may be of service to you and to the State, but of that we will talk later. In the meantime, help me to learn the truth.

I have already attempted to describe my state of mind at the commencement of this talk. As I went on, there came the feeling that, keen as they usually are, the men were having some difficulty in grasping my full meaning; were in doubt whether I really did intend to carry out in all sincerity the plan of actually living their life. But as they began to comprehend the full

10

significance of the idea, their applause increased in volume and heartiness. [1]

I have spoken of the sensitive quickness of the prison audience; I experienced an instance. When the next to the last paragraph of my address was first written, I used the words, "and in the morning looked out at God's sunlight through the same iron bars." Then there had come into my mind the picture made by the grated window, and I added three words so as to read, "looked out at the pieces of God's sunlight." As I spoke those words a burst of hearty laughter at the touch of irony came so quickly that I had to wait before finishing the clause; at the close of the sentence, with its note of brotherhood, all laughter ceased at once; and the loudest applause of the morning showed me that what I had said had struck just the right note, and that the help I wanted from the prisoners would not be lacking.

After my address I leave the Prison and proceed to my office where I am interviewed by representatives of the press. This is a disagreeable duty which I had up to this last moment hoped to escape; for even after giving up the notion of disguise I had still cherished the idea that it was possible, with the aid of the Warden, to keep my adventure from being made public until it was all over. But in our talk this morning the Warden very quickly convinced me that secrecy is impossible.

"Can't you give instructions to all the officers to say nothing about it outside?" I ask.

"Certainly I can," is the Warden's reply; "and you know as well as I just how much good it would do. Here are a hundred officers; they might have the best intentions, but each one would have to confide it to his wife, and she to her dearest friend; and it would be all over town in less than two hours. You must remember that this is a very interesting performance, and you can't keep it quiet. I'll try it if you say so, but my belief is that it would be a mistake. You might better see to it that it gets into the newspapers in the shape you want, rather than let it leak out and be misrepresented, intentionally or otherwise."

The Warden has the old newspaper man's instinct, and reluctantly I have to admit that his view is correct. So without more

---

[1] One of the men in Auburn Prison, explaining the feelings of their inmates in chapel this Sunday morning, writes the following comment: "The men could not realize what was actually meant by this at first; and as they grasped the idea it sort of staggered them and some thought, myself among others, 'What's the matter? What manner of man is this?'"

ado I turn my attention to aiding the press to get what there is, and if possible get it straight. Fortunately the local representative of many important papers is more than usually careful and intelligent. I hand him a copy of my address of this morning and he gets to work. If we cannot have secrecy then let us have all the publicity we can. After all, the newspapers may interest people in my adventure, and thus stimulate an interest in Prison Reform. I am willing to waive my personal preferences if by so doing I can help forward the cause; especially as the satisfaction of my personal preferences is manifestly impossible.

After this I give attention to my private affairs which are arranged for the coming week. Strict orders are issued that no attempt be made to reach me with personal matters of any sort, except in a case of the most extreme importance. I am to be as completely shut off from the world, from my family and friends, as any regular prisoner. So when it comes to this point I begin to feel rather serious. I am aware of a certain sinking at the heart, doubtless a form of fear; the unknown always has terrors.

The plan determined upon with the Warden is that I shall be placed with the Idle Company for the first day or two—those poor fellows whom I have often seen in the prison yard during the past summer, taking their melancholy exercise by marching aimlessly up and down, and occasionally resting by sitting on their buckets; then along about the third day to go to one of the shops—which one to be determined later. But the Warden told me this afternoon that upon mentioning this plan to one of the officials he had protested. "I shouldn't like to have Mr. Osborne put with that Idle Company. They're the toughest bunch of fellows in the Prison."

"That's just what he wants," was the Warden's reply.

It is true, I do want to make acquaintance with the worst as well as the best; but I can't help feeling just a trifle uneasy at the prospect of close relations with the toughest bunch in the Prison; to say nothing of my query as to just how the toughest bunch in the Prison is going to meet me. What will they be like at close range? And, if they do not look with favor upon my action, in what way will their resentment be shown? These questions keep rising to the surface. At the same time, I begin to be aware of an ache in one of my teeth where a filling came out some time ago. Luckily I did not say on just what day my term would begin, although of course I've had to-morrow in mind right along. If my toothache gets worse, I can wait over another day and have it attended to. Perhaps, on the whole it would be best to wait over another day. On the other hand, I have an idea that the toothache is nothing but plain cowardice.

As we sit down to dinner, I attempt to be jocular with my youngest. "Well, Golfer," I remark; "this is my last good meal. To-morrow your father goes to prison for a week!"

"Hm!" responds the interesting youth, "it'll do you good."

I recover myself with some difficulty. "Now what in thunder do you mean by that?"

"Oh, you won't be so fat when you come out."

I'm inclined to think he's right, but it is evident that I need expect no sentimental sympathy from my own family.

Here I close my journal for to-night. I feel decidedly solemn. I wonder how I shall be feeling at this time to-morrow night.

"To-morrow! Why, to-morrow I may be
Myself with yesterday's sev'n thousand years."

CHAPTER III
MONDAY MORNING

Cell 15, second tier, north, north wing, Auburn Prison. September 29. It is noon hour; somewhere about 12:45 I should think.

I am a prisoner, locked, double locked. By no human possibility, by no act of my own, can I throw open the iron grating which shuts me from the world into this small stone vault. I am a voluntary prisoner, it is true; nevertheless even a voluntary prisoner can't unlock the door of his cell—that must be done by someone from outside. I am perfectly conscious of a horrible feeling of constraint—of confinement. It recalls an agonized moment of my childhood when I accidentally locked myself into a closet.

My cell is exactly four feet wide by seven and a half feet long, measuring by my own feet, and about seven and a half feet high.[2] The iron bed is hooked to the wall and folds up against it; the mattress and blankets hang over it. The entire furniture consists of one stool, a shelf or table which

---

[2] Mine was one of the larger cells. Many of them are only three and a half feet wide.

drops down against the wall when not held up by hooks, an iron basin filled with water for washing purposes, a covered iron bucket for other purposes, a tin cup for drinking water which was filled shortly before noon by the convict orderly, and an old broom which stands in the corner. A small wooden locker with three shelves is fastened up in the farther left-hand corner. The pillow hangs in the opposite right-hand corner over the edge of the bed.

This is a cell in one of the oldest parts of the prison. It has a concrete floor and plastered walls and ceiling, and looks clean. From my grated door, being on the second tier, I can see diagonally out of four heavily barred windows in the outer wall, looking across about ten feet, over the open space which drops to the stone corridor below, and rises to the highest galleries. Through the two lower windows I catch glimpses of the ground, through the two upper, of leaves and branches and the sky. The daylight in the cell is enough at the present moment to read and write by, but none too good. Outside it is a very bright, sunny day. If it were a dark day I could not see much without a light. The electric bulb hangs from a hook in the center of the rounded ceiling and my head nearly touches it.

So much for my present surroundings; now let me begin the story of the day.

Upon arising this morning at home, the toothache, although I could still feel it grumbling, had so modified that I became convinced that it was largely imagination. As it has since disappeared it must have been entirely imagination. There seems to be no excuse whatever for not going ahead.

Having noticed yesterday that, although the prisoners are allowed to wear their hair as they please, their faces are all smooth shaven, I begin the day by the sacrifice of my mustache. I shave, dress, and eat as much breakfast as I can—which is not very much.

At nine o'clock I am at the railway station to say good-bye to the Warden, who has been called to Albany on business. After the train leaves at 9:30 I go to my office, where there are some last matters to attend to, bid farewell to the few friends who are about, and at ten o'clock present myself at the prison entrance.

The polite guard at the gate unlocks it, I enter, and the first barrier between me and the world shuts behind me. I mount the steps to the main building, and turn into the Warden's office. I am dressed in old clothes, appropriate for the occasion, and have no valuables or money about my person.

In the Warden's office a few last details are arranged with Grant, the Prison Superintendent of Industries, who is acting for the Warden; and my name and certain details of my family history and career of crime are taken down by the Warden's clerk on a slip of paper, which is handed over to a good-looking, well-groomed young officer, to whom I am given in charge.

On Saturday, when writing out yesterday's address, it occurred to me that it might be useful to take an alias. Such a notion doubtless seems a trifle foolish at first thought; considering that there is no secret of my identity, but I reasoned that if officers and prisoners always had my own name in mind or on tongue every time they looked at or addressed me, it would really make it more difficult to be accepted on the basis of an ordinary inmate. I decided, therefore, to take a name which would have no association whatever with the chairman of the Prison Reform Commission, yet would be somewhat in character. So on the records I am entered as Thomas Brown, No. 33,333x.

The young officer in his neat blue uniform, carrying his loaded stick, says briefly, "Step this way, Brown." I am hazily aware of being a momentary object of interest to the men in the back office; a heavy iron door is unlocked at the head of a flight of iron stairs; and as the door clangs behind me and I hear the key turn in the lock, I begin to realize that I am a prisoner. I have made a bargain with myself to stay here a week, and I cannot leave sooner without serious loss of self-respect.

The taciturn young officer takes me downstairs and across the yard. I am conscious of many pairs of eyes looking out from windows and doors, and the few prisoners scattered about the yard singly or in groups stare with interest. My guide accompanies me to one of the buildings about halfway down on the left, which proves to be the tailor shop. Here in a corner of the shop, without any screens and in full view of all passers in and out, are three porcelain-lined iron bathtubs side by side, looking very white and clean. I am directed to take off my clothes, which I do, and then ordered to get into one of the tubs, in which a negro prisoner has drawn a warm bath. I obey and make use of the soap, and later of the towel which the attendant hands me. After I am dry I am given my prison clothes—a suit of underwear, a pair of socks, a cotton shirt with narrow blue and white stripes, and a suit of rough gray cloth. There is also a pair of very thick and heavy shoes. All the clothes are new. My coat fastens down the front with five light metal buttons, on

15

which are the words State Prison in raised letters. The seven smaller buttons of the waistcoat are similar. My uniform is not exactly a first-class fit, but good enough for the purpose. A cap, rough gray to match the suit, together with a stiff new gray towel and a cake of white soap, completes my outfit. I am ordered to remove my wedding ring, but the officer explains that I am to be allowed to retain it. This is the first exception made in my case.

The rest of my belongings are bundled up and disappear from sight. All that is left of my former self is what can't very well be eradicated. So far as is humanly possible, I am precisely like the other 1,329 gray figures which to-day inhabit this abnormal world within the walls.

We return to the administration building and I am taken to the office of the Principal Keeper, where are propounded to me a series of questions, the answers to which are duly entered on the records: name, age, occupation, married or single, Protestant or Catholic, parents living or dead, any children, character of my crime, is this my first term, have I ever gone under any other name, temperate or intemperate, and so forth and so on. Some of these questions have already been answered at the front office, and the officer holds the paper in his hand; but I answer them again, suppressing such facts as I do not wish to have a matter of record. [3]

After my history has been duly taken, I am handed a copy of the rules of the prison; and the Principal Keeper facing me across a small desk makes a neat little speech, giving friendly advice as to my conduct while in the institution. It is excellent advice, as far as it goes, and for it I thank him respectfully.

Then clearing his throat he says slowly and ponderously, "Brown, after you have had your medical examination, you will be put to work in the basket-shop, under Captain Lamb. He will give you full instructions concerning your place in his company and your work."

It is on the tip of my tongue to say, "But it was all arranged with the Warden that I should be put first with the Idle Company." Fortunately, however, I catch myself just in time. It is not for a convict to offer objections or to argue with the P. K. So I utter another brief but respectful, "Thank you, sir," and feel a certain relief at the postponement of my acquaintance with the "toughest

---

[3] It is perhaps needless to point out how much inaccuracy there must be in any statistics made up from records taken in such a manner. The prisoner gives such answers as he pleases. If he is found out in a lie he is punished—but how often is he found out?

bunch of fellows in the Prison." The Warden returns to-morrow, and an exchange can then be made if it is thought advisable; in the meantime it is my business to do exactly what I am told.

From the Principal Keeper's office I am taken next door to the Chaplain. Here my reception is in marked contrast to the previous official frigidities. I fear that this is partially due to the Chaplain's failure quite to realize that it is only Thomas Brown, a stranger and a new arrival, whom he takes so warmly by the hand. My evident embarrassment evidently embarrasses him, for I am beginning to enter so much into the spirit of the place that I almost feel as if I had been detected in an attempt to conceal my identity. The Chaplain turns me over to a convict stenographer who plies me with another series of questions, and I give my statistics for a third time. I can only hope that my answers to these various sets of questions are fairly uniform, or else that they will not be compared too closely.

The Chaplain and his assistant (a very nice-looking prisoner named Dickinson, whose acquaintance I made yesterday) inquire as to what books I should like to read, and I am shown a typewritten list from which to choose. I am hardly in a mental state to do so, but manage to make a selection. Unfortunately nothing I want seems available; but Dickinson promises to get one of the books later, and in the meantime I am presented with a Bible. Then I am taken upstairs and left with the Doctor.

The Doctor puts me through another series of questions, the fourth; many of them duplicates of the others. Then he starts on a careful physical examination which he does not finish as it is getting too near dinner time. The officer returns for me, and laden with my complete prison baggage—one towel, a cake of soap and a Bible—I am conducted to the north wing, up a short flight of iron stairs and along a narrow wooden gallery with an iron bar for a rail, to my cell on the second tier, Number 15. It has already been described. I remain here while the officer goes to get the small handbag left at the Warden's office, containing a few things which I am to be allowed to have in my cell—writing paper, toothbrush, towels, sponges, toilet paper, and a razor. Most of the men are shaved twice a week by convict barbers in the different shops, and not even the barbers are allowed razors in their cells. As a new man I ought not to be allowed any of these luxuries, but this is exception number two.

The officer first returns with the wrong bag, but soon after with the right one, and I am then locked in until dinner time. Soon my keeper turns up, Captain Lamb, the head of the basket-shop. He introduces himself and then gives me instructions as to my immediate conduct; explains the marching signals, the seating at meals, et cetera. In obedience to his instructions, I take off my cap and coat to leave them in the cell; and when he soon passes along the gallery outside, unlocking the cells by pressing down the levers, I push open the grated door and follow close behind him. At the foot of the iron stairs he allots me a place toward the end of the line; and at the word of command we first shuffle and then march in double file along the stone corridors, and in single file into the mess-hall. As we enter, the Principal Keeper stands at the door. I had been warned to place my right hand on my left breast, by way of salute; but the prisoner behind me, fearing I have forgotten, gives me a friendly poke, and I assume the proper attitude of respect. Our line swings around to the right and marches past row after row of men in gray, all facing in the same direction and bending silently over their food.

Well beyond the center of the room I have a place at the end of a long wooden shelf which forms the table. At a sharp rap of the Keeper's iron-shod stick on the floor, we pull out our stools, and stand again erect; a second rap, we seat ourselves and immediately fall to, as our dinner has been waiting for us. I am pleased and rather surprised to find it, if not hot, at least sufficiently warm. Our bill of fare includes a cup of something presumably meant for coffee; a bowl of a thick liquid (I could not decide whether it was soup or gravy, so I waited to see what the others did with it; some used it for one, some for the other; but it turned out to be very palatable bean soup); a slice or two of very good ham; excellent boiled potatoes; two or three pickles I did not try; and two large thick slices of bread. It was not a bad meal, and had I been hungry I should have done more justice to it.

One of the rules the Captain mentioned is that no bread must be left on the table; so, noticing what the other men do, I watch for the passing of the waiter with a large pail of bread, from which he gives an extra slice to those who want it, and shy my second slice into his pail as he goes by. Of course no conversation is allowed at meals; and anything less appetizing than the rows of gray shoulders and backs of heads in front of one I cannot imagine. The watching keepers, standing sternly and silently by, certainly do not add to the hilarity of the occasion. I am reminded of what my convict friend once said to me, "You know we don't really eat here; we just stoke up."

During the beginning of our meal other companies are continually arriving and taking their places in front of us; and during the latter part others are departing from behind us, accompanied by a curious noise which sounds like the rattling of castanets. I soon make out that it is the disposal of the spoons, forks, and knives. I have been cautioned by the Captain that upon leaving the table the three implements must be held in full view; in my left hand if I march on that side, otherwise in my right. These implements are jealously watched so that a prisoner shall not carry them to his cell and turn them into means of attack, escape, or self-destruction.

At the end of the meal the officer's stick again strikes the stone pavement sharply; we rise, shove our stools back under the table shelf, then fall in line behind another departing company, each man holding aloft his knife, fork, and spoon which he drops into the proper receptacles near the door where a watchful officer keeps careful tally. We march back along the stone corridors, break ranks at the foot of the iron stairs, traverse the narrow gallery, and are soon in our cells where we are locked in; and I begin to write this journal.

It is curious what a resentful feeling overtakes one as that iron grated door swings to and is double locked. I can perfectly imagine a high-strung man battering himself against it from sheer nervousness.

Captain Lamb has just been to the door of my cell again. He begins with a reprimand. "Brown, I noticed you turning around at dinner; that is not allowed. I will let it pass this time, but don't let it happen again. The rule is always, 'Eyes front.'"

"Thank you, sir."

The Captain then gives instructions regarding my next moves. It seems that I am soon to put on coat and cap and march to the shop, taking my bucket if I desire to empty it. The Captain explains that he will first pass along the gallery, unlocking the levers; then almost immediately return, pushing them down, and that when he pushes down my lever I must be ready to press heavily against the door so as to get it open quickly; then follow after the others, and take my place in line. He also gives instructions as to my conduct in the shop. "I call all my men by their first names, so I shall call you Thomas. I allow my company to have some talk in the shop. It is not strictly according to rule; but my men have the reputation of being a little hard to manage, and I find they get along better if I give them some leeway. So you may converse about your work; but you must be careful not to talk loud or create any disorder, and you must shut up at once in case another officer or a visitor comes into the shop. Also you must not leave your place of work without permission."

I again thank the Captain, and say that I will try to mind my own business and not make any more trouble than I can help. He smiles rather a grim smile, and replies dryly that he doesn't think there will be any trouble, and goes away. My time for writing must be nearly up for the present.

Yes! I hear a clicking, beginning at the far-distant end of the gallery around the corner to my left. It draws rapidly nearer and I can hear the key turning in the locks. I have put on my coat and cap. The Captain unlocks my lever and passes along the gallery to the right. He will soon be back, so this writing must be put away in the locker; then I can stand ready and waiting at the door. It would be as well not to expose myself to another reprimand.

There is of course another side to the foregoing story, and that is the advent of Thomas Brown as viewed, not by himself, but by his new companions—the regular inmates of the prison. What did the convicts think of it all?

As it happens, two of them were moved to record their impressions, and their accounts have come to my hands in a roundabout way. I can not do better than supplement my own story by extracts from these papers. I do not know the writers, I do not even know their names, and the stories were written entirely without hint or solicitation from me. It is natural that I should think them interesting; I hope that others may find them so.

Here is A's account:

On Monday, a little after 10 A. M., a man passed through the front gate, and without any ceremony was registered on the book of entries as Tom Brown and recorded as No. 33,333x. After a brief examination he was conducted to the tailor-shop where the cutaway was changed for a suit of prison gray.

The funds of Mr. Brown being at low ebb, the state graciously presented him with a towel, a pair of working shoes, and a red bandanna handkerchief. [4]

With these meager possessions Tom again emerged into the large yard; and the old adage, "What a difference just a few clothes make," became very evident, for in every appearance he looked just like the brotherhood he was about to join.

When a new man enters, a general whisper is always heard throughout the various shops. "Well, here's a new boarder!" This was applied to him as he passed through the yard accompanied by Captain D.

---

[4] The writer is mistaken, for as a matter of fact the state was not so generous; the handkerchief was my own—as was also my toothbrush.—T. M. O.

We all knew who Tom was, but on the Sunday previous when he outlined his intentions a silent compact had been made—to consider him as an ordinary inmate; and the promise was fulfilled to the letter. What our thoughts were—is an entirely different story.

B's account is somewhat more racy and intimate, and contains some very characteristic touches:

A few comments in the cell house on the day of Tom Brown's arrival at Auburn Prison to start his self-imposed bit.

"Hello, Bill! There he goes. And say, he just walks with the confidence of an old timer! Well, old pals, you will have to take your hats off to him as a game one, all right!"

By this time all the keepers in the cell house looking through the windows. But not with that same old smile they usually carry. Someone sung in a low tone that old time melody,

"O what has changed them?"

and the gang had to take to cover; a look from some of the sore keepers made it plain we better move.

While he was down getting dolled up in his new suit of gray, someone asked where the P. K. was; and Jack replied, "Why, he just passed me over in the alley; and say, fellows, he has got so thin I didn't know him; I guess you'll find him over in the jail office hiding behind a broom."

Someone gave us the wire that Tom was coming up the yard again, and we made a bee line for a rubber. Sure enough there is Tom, coming up the line in his new college makeup and a prison towel in his hand. All the boys stood quiet and watched. In fact nine out of ten had a lump in his throat too big to swallow. I must confess I got a cold chill that ran down my back, and it jumped from limb to limb like a cobblestone. Well, after we all came to, "our brave Tom" was locked in his cell, 15-2-N.N.W.; and then the stoolpigeons was put to work to watch who went to speak with him.

These extracts, which are given verbatim, throw interesting sidelights upon the attitude and state of mind of the prisoners—their extreme sensitiveness, their instant response to kindness, real or fancied, their relations to their keepers, their ready cheerfulness and sense of humor. As one can see, there was arising among them at the very outset something quite unexpected—a deep sense of gratitude for what they persisted in thinking a great sacrifice on my part; an eager answer to the sympathy from the outer world which my coming among them typified. The lump in the throat at the first sight of Tom Brown clad as a convict is significant of many things.

The fact that they all greatly exaggerated my personal discomfort and in so many ways gave me credit where none was due, is only an evidence of their hunger for the human relationship, for that sympathy from our fellowmen which we all crave so intensely, and from which convicts are very far from exempt. There is no need to comment further upon these interesting extracts.

It is a real pity that we can not have as well the views of the third party in the affair—the keepers. Frank comment from them would be also most valuable. I only hope that the one who, on a certain occasion, invited and came very near receiving, personal violence by ejaculating, "Damn fool!" behind my back, represented an exception. Unquestionably, however, he did voice a considerable amount of official sentiment within the prison, as well as much unofficial sentiment outside. That was so natural as to be inevitable. There are always those who will misunderstand one's motives and actions, no matter how plain the explanation may be.

CHAPTER IV
MONDAY AFTERNOON

Later in the day; about 5:30, I think; I have no watch and nowhere does there seem to be a clock in sight, so I am necessarily rather vague as to the exact time.

I am again double locked in my cell, this time for the night—fourteen mortal hours.

For me there is plenty to do—to write, to read, to think about; but how about those who do not care for reading, who write with difficulty, or who can neither read nor write? Then again, I look forward to only six nights in this stone vault; but how about those who must look forward to an endless series of nights, month after month, year after year, five, ten, fifteen, twenty years, life?

My God! How do they ever stand it?

Until nine o'clock, when the lights will go out, I am my own master; my own master in a world of four feet by seven and a half, in which I am the only inhabitant. Other human beings are living all about—on either side, at the back, above, below; yet separated by double thick stone walls from every other living creature in this great community, I am

22

absolutely solitary. I have never felt so curiously, desperately lonely. The loneliness in the midst of crowds is proverbial; but the loneliness in the midst of a crowd of invisible human beings—not one of whom do you even hear—that has in it an element of heavily weighted horror which is quite indescribable. It can only be felt.

The curious sensation of nervous resentment, noticed this noon, is upon me in greater force to-night. If I were to just let myself go, I believe I should soon be beating my fists on the iron grated door of my cage and yelling. Of course I shall do nothing so foolish, but I feel the impulse distinctly. I wonder how I shall stand a week of this. I must certainly keep my nerves under better control, at present they are quivering at the slightest sound.

This has certainly been one of the most interesting days of my life, and the afternoon more interesting than the morning. I wish I could describe it adequately.

The interval between dinner and the march to the shop is occupied chiefly by writing this journal; but I also have a pleasant call from the Chaplain's assistant, Dickinson. He does not bring me the book I selected this morning, but in its place another book and some magazines, for none of which do I care. What I do care about is the pleasant chat we have. Not many words have been exchanged before he drops the books he is engaged in distributing along the cells and dashes off; soon returning with photographs of his wife and three charming children. He himself is a clean-cut, fine-looking fellow, with honest blue eyes and a good face—not a single trace of the "Criminal" about him. He tells me some of the details of his story, and it is a sad one. But his imprisonment is now over; he expects to go out on Saturday. Some time ago he was granted his parole on condition of obtaining a job, and that he has now secured. He says this prison experience has been a "good lesson" to him. I have no doubt it has, nor that his hopes will be fulfilled; but the pity of it! Why should not a man like this, guilty of only a lesser crime, guiltless of criminal intent, be allowed to go on parole under suspended sentence, and not have to come to prison at all? Why should not he and his wife and children have been spared these long years of separation, this bitter degrading experience, this almost irreparable stain upon his name?

At about half past one o'clock the cells are unlocked, as I have already described. The Captain returns, pressing down the levers; I push open my door, place my tin cup on a small shelf at the left on

23

leaving the cell and follow the other men rapidly along the narrow gallery and down a short flight of narrow, slippery iron stairs, coming to a halt at the door opening into the yard. Here the Captain places me third in line on the left, for we march in double file. I am flattered by the promotion, but possibly the man in front of me feels differently about it. I hope he'll bear no grudge; but, if he had turned about and landed me one between the eyes that last time I trod on his heel, it would not have been surprising. The shoes presented me by the state of New York are so stiff and clumsy that I find it quite a task to manage my feet; it is difficult to steer them properly; and of course this marching in close order is something quite new to me.

First at half speed—then at a good round pace—we march out of the north wing, wheel to the right on reaching the center walk, swing down the length of the yard; then turn to the left, pass through the building where the buckets are emptied and washed, and halt where they are placed to dry and be disinfected. After a pause here of only a moment we march on again to the basket-shop.

Just as we reach there and break ranks, the young officer who served as guide this morning presents himself; and in silence I am conducted back up the yard and again to the Doctor's office, where my very thorough medical examination is completed.

After the Doctor is through with me I go to the hallway outside his office where a number of other prisoners are awaiting their turns. As my officer has not come back, and does not do so for some time, there is an opportunity to practice what is apparently the most necessary virtue of prison life—patience. I take my place along the wall with the other convicts and watch for a chance to open a whispered conversation. From where I stand I can look up a short flight of steps into the front room of the hospital, where there are a number of men moving about; among them one of the city undertakers. Then I remember having heard at the front office, as I came in this morning, of the sudden death of a young prisoner last night from pneumonia. Four convicts come up the stairs, bringing a large, ominous looking, oblong receptacle, which they take to a door on my left. It does not look quite like a coffin, but there is little doubt as to its purpose. As the door is opened, I glance in; and there, covered with a white sheet, is all that remains of the poor lad—the disgraced and discarded human tenement of one divine spark of life.

A death in prison. Tears fill my eyes as I turn away thinking of that lonely, friendless deathbed; thinking that perhaps some loving mother or young wife in the world outside, bearing bravely her own

24

share of shame and punishment, has been struggling to keep body and soul together until her prisoner could come back home; perhaps at this very moment wondering why she has not received from him the last monthly letter. And now—— Can the world hold any tragedy more terrible than this?

A young negro prisoner standing by, who has also looked into the chamber of death, breathes a low sigh and whispers, "God! That's where I wish I was!"

The convict next him, a broad-shouldered young chap, who whispers to me that he comes from Brooklyn and gets out in January, goes in to ask some special favor of the Doctor. He gives me on the side a most humorous and quite indescribable wink and grin as his request is granted. His attitude suggests that he has "slipped one over" on somebody. He mounts the steps to the hospital and the young negro takes his turn with the Doctor as the coffin, heavy now with its mournful load, is brought out from the room on the left. At the same moment the officer returns to my rescue; and I follow him downstairs and out into the fresh air and the sunlight.

Comedy and tragedy seem to jostle each other in prison even as in the world outside. But the comedy itself is tragic; while the tragedy lies beyond the realm of tears—in the gray twilight region of a suffering too deep for speech, where sympathy seems helpless.

As I now sit writing in my cell, from out the darkness, loneliness, and stillness about me comes the sweet voice of a violin. Someone is playing the melody of Mendelssohn's Spring Song, and playing well. I wonder if he knows that I am near him, and is trying to send me his message of good will. One peculiarity of this place is that sounds reach the heavily recessed door of a cell mainly by reflection from the outer wall, and my ear is not sufficiently trained to know from what direction the sounds come. The invisible violinist, wherever he is, has an unusually good tone and plays with genuine feeling. Unfortunately he has not played many bars before more instruments join in—jewsharps, harmonicas, and other things. It is an extraordinary jumble of sounds—a wild pandemonium after the deadly quiet of a few moments ago. A train blowing off steam at the New York Central station, immediately opposite our front windows, is also contributing its quota of noise.

The gallery boy has just passed along, filled my tin cup with water for the night, and exchanged a few words. He says that for twenty minutes each evening, from six-forty to seven, each man may "do what he likes" in his cell. A cornet is the latest addition to the noise. The whole episode impresses me as being such a mingling of the pathetic and the humorous that I don't know whether to laugh or cry. Consider the conditions which make twenty minutes of such a performance a boon to man!

The gallery boy evinces a desire to strike up friendly relations; he brings me a box of matches in case I want to smoke, and offers to do anything for me he can. I am not a smoker, but I don't like to decline his good offices; so I stow away the matches for future reference.

Let me resume the thread of my story.

The officer takes me from the Doctor's office to the room where the Bertillon measurements are taken. Here there is a fifth set of questions to answer. I have not the slightest possible objection to giving all the statistics the state officials want; my time is theirs, and there is no possible hurry. I may as well get rid of a few hours, more or less, of my "bit" in this way as in any other; so I shall not register any kick even if I am called upon to supply fifty sets of statistics instead of only five.

The orders of the Bertillon clerk are given perfunctorily, with the air of one who is greatly bored by the whole performance. Naturally it is not so novel to him as to me. I remove my coat and put on, as they are handed to me by the assistant, a white linen shirt-bosom, a very dirty collar of the requisite size, and a black coat and necktie. Then I am photographed—front view and profile. The use of the peculiar apparel is, presumably, either to make the photograph clearer, or to have all "subjects" taken under similar conditions and looking somewhat as they do when out of prison and in ordinary clothes.

Then my finger tips, on both hands, are carefully rolled one by one in India ink, and impressions of them taken on cards—twice separately, and twice all five at once. This seems to bore the clerk more than the photographing.

Then a series of measurements from top to toe is taken, and every possible means of identification noted and registered: color of hair and eyes; shape of head; characteristics of eyes, nose, mouth; the scar received at football thirty-four years ago, which I supposed was successfully concealed by my right eyebrow; the minute check on the left ear from a forgotten frostbite; the almost imperceptible bit of smooth skin on the back of my right hand, where a small lump was once removed by electricity; no blemish or defect is over-looked—until I begin to feel like a sort of monstrosity. I derive some satisfaction, however, from the fact that my business-like inquisitor

26

is quite at a loss to account for six peculiar scars upon my upper left arm, familiar to Harvard men of my generation. It is some satisfaction to know that my Alma Mater has not sent many of her sons to take a post-graduate course in this institution.

So complete and searching have been the examination and record for identification that I have a sort of discouraged feeling about the future. It occurs to me that I may be cramped in a choice of further activities; and that my chance of ever gaining a good living by honest burglary has been considerably reduced, if not destroyed. I communicate this rather frivolous sentiment to the clerk who receives it grimly, and is more bored than ever. I feel properly snubbed and rebuked.

Evidently a prisoner should speak only when spoken to, and certainly should not venture to joke with an official. I shall take warning and not offend again.

I wonder how my measurements differ from those of the average criminal, and how much of a rough-neck my photograph will make me look.

At last all preliminaries are completed; and now I am free to consider myself a full-fledged convict.

The young officer who up to now has been my guide and philosopher, if not exactly a friend, conducts me down the yard once again, duly delivers me over to Captain Lamb at the basket-shop, and takes his final departure. The Captain leads me at once to a rough wooden table, about thirty feet in front of the raised platform on which he sits. Here stands a good-sized, broad-shouldered, black-haired fellow, working with his back to us as we approach. He pauses as we stop before his table.

"Jack," says the Captain, "this is Thomas Brown. Thomas, this is John Murphy, who will be your working partner."

"Glad to meet you, Mr. Brown," says a pleasant voice.

Looking toward my partner and his outstretched hand, I decide to venture another joke. "Captain," I remark, advancing my hand cautiously, "this may be all right; but it's only fair to warn you that if this gentleman is any relative of the Boss of Tammany Hall there may be trouble."

A pair of honest gray eyes light up with a smile as the owner says, "No, Mr. Brown, I'm no relation; and what's more I haven't any use for him."

Upon this we shake hands cordially. "Excuse me, Captain," I remark to that officer, "but you see I want to be careful and not run into difficulties of any kind."

The Captain smiles gravely in his turn, and introduces me to

27

another of the prisoners who has approached at a sign from the officer. He is a slightly built, pleasantly smiling young man who is to be my boss in the shop, Harley Stuhlmiller. By him I am to be initiated into the art of making basket bottoms; and Murphy is to have me as his partner or apprentice, and see that I make no mistakes in following the boss's instructions.

So I take off my cap and coat and start to work. I do not find it very difficult; for, curiously enough, over forty years ago I learned something of the art of weaving baskets. When I was a young lad my family spent a summer at a place on the New England seacoast. On the beach was the tent of an old Indian, who made and sold baskets; and, having much time on my hands, I persuaded the old fellow to teach me basket-making. One certainly never knows when an odd bit of knowledge or information may come handy; here am I making use of something learned two generations and more ago, and never practiced since.

I spend a really pleasant afternoon learning my job and chatting under my breath with the two men—my boss and my partner. They give me some wise advice as to my conduct, some information as to prison ways, and compliment me upon the quickness with which I pick up the basket work. I explain about the previous experience and tell them not to give me too much taffy. They assure me that what I have done in the short time I have been working is really very good. The expected task for a man and his partner is five bottoms a day, and I accomplish one and a half for a part of the afternoon. Stuhlmiller calls this to the attention of John, the citizen instructor, and he smilingly grunts approval, but suggests certain improvements in my manner of work. Thus, so far as the shop is concerned, I seem to be a success. The convicts about me pay very little attention to the newcomer, but I catch an occasional smile and nod of encouragement.

Along in the afternoon, about four o'clock I should judge, work begins to slack up; and several of the prisoners who have finished their allotted tasks are walking back and forth. Each one confines himself to such a very short distance, that I inquire of Murphy the reason; and he tells me that the boundaries of each man's walk are the posts of the building on either side of his bench or table. This gives a very restricted area for exercise, but, as it is the only chance for exercise at all, the men make the most of it.

At about half past four my partner proposes that we knock off work and clean up. By this time there is a general cessation of labor about the shop, and most of the men are sweeping up around their tables and benches. Murphy produces a broom, and informs me

28

that when two men work together it is customary to take turns in cleaning up after work-hours. So at this hint I take the broom and soon have the work done. Then we wash up; my partner sharing with me his soap and towel. I put on my coat and cap and await further developments.

Murphy, after replacing the soap and towel in his locker, comes around to my side of our workbench or table. "Say, Brown," he remarks, "I hope you won't think me imposing on you in any way, but while we work together I intend to treat you as if I had never seen or known of you before."

"Thank you, Murphy," I reply, pleased at his frankness, "that is exactly the way I want to be treated."

Certainly nothing could be better than the attitude of the two men with whom my work has brought me in contact. There has been not the slightest tinge of self-consciousness; no trace of servility or currying favor, absolutely nothing except Murphy's frank explanation to make me feel that they are not treating me exactly as I asked them yesterday to do—as a new man and one of themselves.

After we have sat around patiently and wearily for a considerable time, the hour for return to the cell-house arrives. The Captain gives the signal to fall in. "Good night, Brown!" "Good night, Murphy!" and I take my place in the line. The Captain counts us with care while we stand rigidly before him. Then the cripples, invalids and poor old broken-down men start ahead of the main body to hobble wearily back to their cells. Meanwhile we able-bodied men of the company march over to the stands where the buckets are drying, pause for an instant, then swing up through the yard, with a tramp, tramp, tramp, that is quite exhilarating after an afternoon's work in the shop.

We march straight up the yard and into the basement door of the main building where, just within the entrance, are placed some tables laden with slices of bread. Following the example of the other men, I grab a slice—some take two slices, there is apparently no restriction as to amount—and then climb the slippery iron stairs in my heavy shoes. As we go along the gallery the man just behind me whispers, "Well, Tom, how do you like it?"

I turn and whisper laughingly, "All right, no kick coming," and turn into my cell.

On the iron shelf outside stands my tin cup filled with a hot black liquid—whether tea or coffee I don't know. What I do know is that the odor is vicious. I hesitate about taking it into the cell.

The gallery boy arriving says, "Brown, I didn't know whether you wanted tea or water, so I gave you tea."

"Thank you," I rejoin, "but I think I'll take water." So he brings back my tin cup filled with a liquid which if mild is comparatively harmless, and at least does not smell to heaven. I enter my cell, which is shut and locked.

After a light breakfast, a lighter dinner, and the afternoon's work, I feel ravenously hungry—so hungry that the bread and water actually taste rather good, even if the bread is sour. To my surprise I make away with the whole slice, dipping each mouthful into the water and eating as I write; for I have at once taken up this journal to chronicle the events of the afternoon while they are still in mind.

I wonder what those greedy children at home will have for dinner to-night. Or whether they will think of this poor, hungry prisoner, eating his lonely bread and water. This morning my eldest remarked cheerfully, "Well, of course we can telephone you any time." How little does he realize the reality.

We used to laugh when in "Pinafore" they sang:

> "He'll hear no tone
> Of the maiden he loves so well;
> No telephone
> Communicates with his cell."

I reminded the young man of those lines this morning.

No, I fear there are few of us who reflect very much upon what is remote from our direct line of vision. But there will be at least one of us who will do considerable reflecting—after this experience.

I certainly do feel hungry!

As a supplement to the foregoing, our friends, A and B, have some further interesting passages:

A: About the first thing an apprentice learns here is the military step; so a few of us watched the company to which Tom was assigned as they passed through the yard from the mess-hall to the shop. As Tom marched by, it became evident from his brisk step that he either learned it at a military academy or had served time in another "institution." [5]

The routine of prison life, which possesses its good, bad and indifferent parts, can hardly be described here. Suffice to say Tom adhered to it for an entire week.

This is what B has to say:

---

[5] For fear that I may be condemned upon purely circumstantial evidence, I hasten to state that neither of these suppositions is correct.—T. M. O.

30

Tom Brown's bed was brought upon the third gallery, cell 55, N.W.; and then in less than fifteen minutes it was changed again, taken down to cell 15, N.N.W. Well, this made the gallery man on the third feel a little blue, for he thought he would like to have Tom on his gallery; and we began to kid him regarding his tough luck.

Well, to make this long story short, the gallery men had their own troubles. Every second man wanted us to drop a note in Tom Brown's cell. But the stools watched; and me, for one, would take no chance. If he got all the notes that was meant for him he would have no room for his bed in his cell.

Well, when he left the cell house that day, after dinner, when he got in line with the rest of the cons he marched down the yard like a major. And make out the cons didn't feel good! And make out the keepers didn't feel blue!

The keepers wouldn't look at Tom when he was looking their way; but after he passed, yog—yog—what a rubbering he got!

So this was the way of the cell house for one whole week; and, believe me, it was some week, indeed.

They tell me when he got in the shop Jack Murphy handed him a broom. You know Jack can be funny when he wants to be. Now the question in mind is, "Did Jack give him that broom to clean out the shop, or did he mean the whole place needed a cleaning out?" Well, I guess Jack, himself, will have to slip us that answer.

CHAPTER V
THE FIRST NIGHT

Still Monday, but later in the evening. The hour is about—but why attempt to specify the exact time? In this place there seems to be no time—only eternity.

Having finished in my journal the account of this afternoon's occurrences, I shall continue to chronicle the events of this evening as long as the light holds out, or as long as there is anything to write about. So I begin where I left off in the last chapter, just after being locked in for the night, as I sat writing and eating my evening meal of bread and water.

I receive a call from Captain Lamb after he has carefully counted all his men and locked us in for the night. As he turned the key in my lock, I was instructed to stand up with both hands on the door and rattle it violently, to show that it was firmly secured. The Captain is very pleasant, and grows quite confidential, telling about his experiences in the regular army in the Philippines. He also explains something of his ideas in regard to handling convicts. Before going away he says that, if I should be taken sick in the night, I must rattle the door and the officer on guard will come and take me to the hospital if necessary.

He goes away and I begin to have that feeling of lonesome desolation I have already attempted to describe. There are some noises; but they are the noises of tramping feet above, below, of clanging bars and grating locks, then of stealthy footfalls and distant doors. Of the many companions who are living all about me I can see no sight—hear no sound. If my cell were big enough, I should walk round and round as I have seen the caged animals do in menageries. As it is, if I get up from writing, I can only hang at my grated door, looking aimlessly out. It grows dark and ever darker in the corridor outside; there are few sounds now. Inside my cell the electric bulb gives barely light enough to read by. It is horribly lonesome.

Looking up from writing, I give a start at the sight of a white face and the figure of a man just outside the grated door. Peering out through the bars, so that I can get the light on his face, I recognize the Chaplain. He puts two fingers through the door, the nearest possible approach to a handshake, and I feel really grateful for a kindly touch and the sound of a friendly voice. I am conscious of an almost insane desire to talk, to pour forth words, as if the bars of my cell were damming back the powers of speech.

The Chaplain is anxious to know how I am getting along, and cheers me by saying that all the men are greatly interested and pleased. "They understand what you are trying to do for them, and appreciate it," he says. Then he tells of one prisoner he has just left in his cell on one of the upper tiers, whom he found reading Schopenhauer. "He said he did not know you, has nothing at all to ask of you, and will probably never see you to speak to; but your action in coming here has somehow made him feel that the pessimistic view he has had of the world must be wrong."

After some further talk, the Chaplain says "Good night," and goes away. I sincerely hope that he is right in his belief; that the men do care; that, besides gaining the information I came here for, my visit may be of some interest and comfort to these poor fellows. Murphy said to me to-day, "Say, you've got the boys all right." If he

32

and the Chaplain are correct, I may get from my experience much more than I expected.

I have already told how, not very long after the Chaplain leaves me and as I sit writing, the lovely sound of a violin floats into the cell. Then come the sounds of many other instruments, and the noise of the train at the railway station, over the wall and across the street. I have also described the ensuing pandemonium. After twenty minutes of these evidences of the human life existing all around, the noise ceases as suddenly as it began, and there comes a silence more profound than that which preceded the musical explosion. Only an occasional cough, the sound of a stealthy footfall, the jar of some iron door or the clank of distant bolt or bar. Yet I am conscious of one curious sound which I am unable to place or explain. It is like a very delicate clicking upon iron and is almost continuous. I wonder whether it is the tapping of prisoners' messages from cell to cell, of which I have heard. It would be convenient to know the telegraphic code, so as to take part in any such conversation. I listen with interest to the clicking, but it seems not to change its direction and to have but little regularity. I wonder what it is.

The night officer has just stopped for a moment at the grating of my cell. I ask him the time. Seven-twenty. Good Lord! I thought it must be nearly nine. I am usually very good at guessing time, but in this place I am utterly unable to make any accurate calculation. Just for the experience, I'm going to stop writing and lock up my writing materials, to see how it feels to have nothing to do.

I take down my paper and pencil again to record a most thrilling discovery. I have found—a pocket in my prison coat! All day I have worried at the absence of one; now I find it—left, on the inside. Imagine the state of mind when such a thing really produces almost a feeling of nervous excitement.

I simply must keep on writing out of sheer desperation. I have tried to use up some minutes by rearranging my clothes, pulling up my socks, and tightening my belt; I have not yet investigated the workings of my bed, as I wish to leave that for a later excitement.

From the distance I catch the single stroke of the City Hall bell, which marks eight o'clock. Another hour yet before the lights go out; and then ten hours more before I can leave this cell!

How in the world do they bear it—the men who look forward to long years of imprisonment? My working partner, Murphy, has a life term. For what, I wonder? He seems like such a good fellow; and the Chaplain has just spoken of him most highly.

What a mystery it all is! And what a commentary on our

33

civilization that we can do nothing better with such men than to throw away their lives and ruin them, body and soul. The old ones arouse one's pity; but the young men—many of those in chapel yesterday were mere boys.

God! What a miserable, shameful waste of human life—of human energy! Must we not find some way in which the good there is in these broken lives can be repaired and made useful to society?

At last a bell, the first signal for the night. I think it is twenty minutes before nine. As the kindly gallery boy has brought me a glass tumbler, I brush my teeth with a minimum of inconvenience, wash my face, and then investigate the workings of the bed. It is loosely fastened to two iron hooks in the wall, on the inside; and the outside rests on two legs which dangle in the air vaguely, and will probably let me down in the night if they do not rest firmly on the floor to begin with. After manipulating the bed successfully, I let down the mattress on top of it and arrange the blankets as well as possible.

About a quarter of an hour more before lights out. It is all very well to look forward to that landmark, but what after that? What of the ten-hour night ahead of me? And this is only the first night of six. Suppose it were the first night of six thousand.

I hastily take a sheet of paper, mark off a space for each day and each night I expect to be here, and scratch off Monday. One-twelfth of my penance gone at any rate. I don't count Sunday, because that will be only half a day; or I will write in Sunday at the bottom, as a sort of separate affair. I hang this rough calendar upon the wall; and then it suddenly occurs to me that it is exactly what I have always read of prisoners doing.

Oh! Will these lights never go out!

I shall put away this writing, and just wait.

Merciful God! How do they ever stand it?

Tuesday morning: after breakfast.

The first night is over. They all say it is the worst. It could hardly be called a success—considered as a period of rest and refreshment; at least it did not "knit up the raveled sleeve of care" to any very great extent. At nine o'clock the lights at last went out. I was already in bed and waiting, but I was not at all prepared for the shock I received. While there is light in the cell, the bars of the door look gray against the darkness outside—and that is bad enough; but when the lights go out, there is just enough brightness from the corridor below to change the door into a grating of most terrible, unearthly blackness. The bars are so black that they seem to close in

34

upon you—to come nearer and nearer, until they press upon your very forehead. It is of no use to shut your eyes for you know they are still there; you can feel the blackness of those iron bars across your closed eyelids; they seem to sear themselves into your very soul. It is the most terrible sensation I ever experienced. I understand now the prison pallor; I understand the sensitiveness of this prison audience; I understand the high nervous tension which makes anything possible. How does any man remain sane, I wonder, caged in this stone grave day after day, night after night?

And always there come the sound of keys turning and the grating of iron hinges and bolts and bars. And as if the double-locked levers were not enough, I noticed for the first time last night a triple lock. A long iron bar drops down in front of all the cells on the tier; and against that iron bar rest the ends of iron brackets projecting from the iron doors. So that by merely unlocking and pressing down the levers you cannot be set free; the long bar must be raised at the end of the gallery, where it is fastened by another lock and special key. This discovery seems to put the crowning touch to that desperate sensation of confinement. I already hate the levers; I doubly hate the lock and big key; but no words can express my detestation of that iron bar.

However, just before ten o'clock I did manage to lose consciousness; I recall the time by the sounds of the nine-fifty New York Central train. Even in the midst of my discomfort I had to smile at the plight of one who has to tell time by trains on the Auburn branch of the New York Central. I do not know how much I slept through the night, but I was greatly disturbed by the frequent and pathetic coughing, sighing, and groaning from other cells. It was only too evident that many others were sleeping no better than I. Possibly the delicate attentions of the night keeper going his rounds and flashing his electric bull's-eye through the bars straight in our faces, may have had something to do with it. Certainly that custom is hardly conducive to unbroken slumbers. Apparently, it is considered necessary to do this in order to prevent suicides. One poor fellow had tried to make away with himself on the previous night; such attempts are not uncommon, I'm told.

Again—what a commentary!

As I had not yet quite reached the point of self-destruction, the flashlight was distinctly annoying; it seemed always to come just after I had succeeded in dropping off to sleep.

And ever, as I started awake again, the blackness of those horrible bars against the faintly lighted corridor!

At last, through one of the upper windows in the outer wall, I detect the faint gray light of the coming dawn. Each time I open my eyes and sit up in bed the small piece of sky to be seen through the grated door of my cell seems a shade less dark; and at last I begin to feel that, after all, perhaps God has not forsaken the world. As the sky grows still brighter, I can distinguish the green of the trees outside; and within, the blackness and the shadows gradually fade away, and the terrible oppression of the night gives place to the confidence of a new day. I listen with a relief that is almost pleasure to the familiar sounds of the six-o'clock factory whistles; and the faithful old bell which has rung for fifty years at the Osborne Works, and which I think I should recognize if I were to hear it in Central Africa.

I partially dress, and then fold up my bed and arrange the mattress and blankets over it, so as to get more room for further evolutions. The night ache in my head is rather bad at first, but cold water on my face and the back of my neck revives me greatly; and by the time my toilet is completed and I am ready for the fray, I feel more nearly like myself. Before I am fully dressed and ready, the lights are switched on, about six-thirty, I judge; and soon the sounds of keys and iron hinges and bars and bolts are heard again; and the noise of shuffling feet in the corridor below tells that the day's routine has begun. [6]

The first night has been worse than I expected; and I dare say it will be the worst of all, unless I find the punishment cells—— However, I am not yet quite certain that I shall try those.

Sufficient unto the day is the evil of the night before. I must throw off the shadows and get a fresh hold. After all, in some ways it might have been worse: the air in my cell was good; I had more blankets than I needed; my bed was not very uncomfortable; and there were no vermin. This last was really what I dreaded most. My cell is clean and well ventilated; surely those are blessings which ought to counterbalance much else.

So I start the new day with courage and undiminished interest in my great experiment.

One of my fellow prisoners, whose comment I quoted in Chapter II, makes the following statement about the condition of the cells at Auburn. "The cells on the second and basement tiers smell fairly well; but in summer the stench from some of the cells is

---

[6] I have since learned that I committed a breach of the rules every morning; one which laid me open to punishment. Men who awake before six-thirty must stay in bed until the bell rings.

terrible." Due, of course, to long use, no sewage, and no proper system of ventilation. In most of the cells the small square hole which opens into some crude sort of ventilating flue has long ago been plugged to prevent the inroads of vermin.

I seem to have been very fortunate in having a cell where discomfort was reduced to a minimum.

The condition of some of the cells I have seen in Sing Sing Prison is unspeakably bad. They are close, dark, damp, foul. To call them unfit for human habitation is to give them undeserved dignity; they are unfit for pigs.

CHAPTER VI
TUESDAY MORNING

In my cell, after dinner; Tuesday, September 30.

At about seven o'clock this morning the long iron bar, which locks the whole tier, is raised; and the Captain pauses a moment at my cell.

"Good morning, Thomas, how did you get through the night?"

"I didn't sleep very well, sir."

"They seldom do the first night. How are you feeling now?"

"Well, fairly good third rate, thank you, sir."

He leaves me; but soon returns along the gallery, unlocking the levers as he comes. Immediately after him walks his trusty, one of the gallery boys, pressing down the levers and letting us out of the stone caves where we have spent the long night. I breathe a sigh of relief and satisfaction as I swing open the iron grating and come out upon the comparative freedom of the gallery.

Each man grasps with his left hand the handle of his heavy iron bucket filled with the slops and sewage of the night. I do the same; and steady my steps by running my right hand along the iron rail as I hurry down the gallery after the others. It is a long journey to the farther stairs, but it is made cheerful by the smiles on the upturned faces of the prisoners in the corridor below. When I have taken my place in line at the foot of the iron stairs, I find further satisfaction in the nods and winks of encouragement from the men gathered about the doorway, at whom I glance as much as I can without turning my head. I rest my heavy bucket on the ground while waiting for the company to complete its formation, taking meanwhile deep breaths of the refreshing morning air. It is another beautiful, sunny autumn day as we look out into the yard.

A sharp rap of the Captain's stick on the stone pavement, and we stand at attention, the handle of each man's bucket in his right hand. Two more quick raps, and we "short-step" out of the building and then "full-step" down the yard. Our route is the same as that of yesterday afternoon. We meet many other companies returning. We march down to the extreme southwest corner of the prison inclosure where is the small brick building which serves as a sewage disposal plant. It seems to be very well arranged for its purpose. As we reach there our ranks divide, entering by two doors, and we march through almost at full speed. I watch my comrades and do exactly as they do; remove the bucket cover upon entering the building; empty the contents into a large circular stone basin, or hopper, into which a stream of water is constantly pouring; pass on quickly to a second basin and fill my bucket at its stream of water; rinse the bucket as I walk along and discharge the contents into a third stone basin with its third stream of running water. It must be confessed that there is a minimum of smell and nastiness; but what a medieval system! The sewage of 1,400 men simply dumped into the river, which flows just outside the walls, and carried along to poison all the towns and villages downstream.

After thus emptying and rinsing the buckets we leave them to be disinfected, aired and dried, upon some wooden racks where each company has its allotted place. Then we march back up the yard, meeting many other companies laden with their buckets on the way down. The march back is very pleasant and I wish it were longer, as exercise in the fresh air and sunlight seems to soothe the tired nerves. By the time we are back at the north wing I am feeling in good condition and ravenously hungry.

Arrived at the cell I have another call from Captain Lamb. I have found him very pleasant and intelligent; and his men, so far as I can yet judge, seem to like him. He has some excellent ideas, and tells me that he would like to give his company setting-up exercises as he once did; but he abandoned them as he received no encouragement; on the contrary it was considered that they were subversive of discipline. This awful fetich, discipline. We most of us do so love it—for others.

Why does it not occur to somebody in authority that the first and best means of getting real discipline, in the sense of good conduct, is to give these men exercise? Here they live, standing or sitting listlessly at their work all day, and shut in their narrow cells fourteen hours at night, with no chance to work off their superfluous energies and keep themselves in proper physical condition. The result in very many cases must be steady degeneration, not only of body, but of mind and soul as well.

The Captain tells me that before breakfast I should clean out my cell; so after he leaves me I carry out his instructions with the assistance of the old broom in the corner. I sweep the dust out of the cell into a corner of the entrance; and the lever locks me back into the cell as I shut the door after the job is completed.

This has not been long done before the clicking of the levers begins again in the distance. Every time we march to meals the clicking begins around the corner to my left and we march to the right; every time we go to the shop the clicking begins on my right and we march to the left. I am beginning to catch on to these various complications. Also to learn the etiquette of dress. When we go to breakfast we wear coats but no caps; to the shop, both caps and coats; to dinner, neither. Waistcoats seem to depend upon the taste and fancy of the wearer. I have worn mine, so far, only in the evening—for warmth.

Marching to breakfast I find myself by the side of a young fellow who is conspicuous among the prisoners by the use of a blue shirt with collar and necktie. He is tall and good-looking, with an air of refinement which is appealing.

I make no breaks upon the march. I shuffle my feet along the stone corridor like the rest, as we move slowly forward; letting other companies who have the right of way go in ahead of us. Then when our turn comes we march more rapidly, changing to single file as we near the mess-room. As the Captain has directed me, I fall in behind my blue-shirted companion and have my right hand on my left breast in ample time to salute the P. K. who, as at yesterday's dinner, stands at the entrance to the mess-hall.

Arrived at my place, which is now in the center of one of the long shelves or tables, I find waiting for me a large dish of oatmeal porridge, a bowl one-third full of the thinnest of skimmed milk, two thick slices of bread, and a cup of the dark fluid we had yesterday and which is supposed to be coffee, but which I learn is called "bootleg" by the prisoners—presumably because old boots is the only conceivable source of its taste and smell. Judging by the samples I've had, the hypothesis does not seem untenable. The taste is quite as bad as the smell, as it is drunk without milk or sugar, and there is no escape from drinking some of it, as it is the only liquid on the table. The bread is known as "punk"—a name not so strikingly appropriate as the other.

I can see no excuse for bad coffee; for good coffee can be made in large quantities, as some railroad refreshment rooms can testify. Tea is a different matter. I do not believe that good tea can be made except in small quantities. If I were to suggest to the prison authorities, it would be cocoa instead of tea, and coffee should be drinkable at least.

George, one of the gallery boys, has presented me this morning with a small package of sugar wrapped in newspaper; but, before I have a chance of deciding whether it is safe to transfer it from my pocket to the oatmeal, my friend in the blue shirt, seated on my left, slides a small yellow envelope toward me. I turn my eyes and head sufficiently to see him. He is staring straight ahead of him, and without moving his lips or a muscle of his face gives a low whisper, "Sugar." I turn back my head and in a voice as low as I can manage and with my lips moving as little as possible mutter, "Thank you." I have had my first introduction to the motionless language of the prisoners.

The sugar makes the oatmeal palatable, and I breakfast very well on that and the bread soaked in what milk I have left over from the porridge. I had forgotten the rule about no bread being left on the table until my new friend reminds me of it by pointing to my two slices and then to the approaching waiter. I promptly toss one of my slices into that functionary's bucket as he passes by, and go on with my breakfast. I feel guilty in taking my neighbor's sugar, when I have some of my own in my pocket, but reflect that mine can be saved for another occasion and shared with him. I find myself wondering if the sugar I'm eating has been honestly come by. Not that I suspect my blue-shirted friend of doing anything wrong; but I am quite sure that in my present condition of mind I should enjoy it better if I knew it had been stolen. I feel as though I would gladly annex almost anything from the state of New York that I could lay my hands on, provided I could do so without too much risk of getting caught. I hope it will be considered that I am not now condoning dishonesty; I am merely trying to explain a state of mind.

The silent meal finished, we return to our cells, where I now have a call from my friend in the blue shirt. It seems that he is a trusty of the "box office"; and has charge of the orders for groceries and their distribution, and his name is Roger Landry. Each convict is allowed to spend three dollars a month in groceries, tobacco and other luxuries—that is if he is fortunate enough to have that amount of money to his credit. As his wages, at one cent and a half a day— the regular rate—could only amount to thirty-seven and a half cents a month, it is obvious that a prisoner must have some outside

40

resources to allow him to spend three dollars. So the prisoners who are better off outside the prison have the luxuries when they get inside; and the poor fellow who has nothing can get nothing. It seems to be a rather literal rendering of the Scripture, "To him who hath shall be given." Certainly from him who hath not is taken away about everything possible—his liberty, his capacity to earn money, his family, friends, and incidentally his self-respect.

The way in which a man's family and friends are taken away seems superlatively cruel. A prisoner gets no wages for his work except his board, lodging, clothes, and the ridiculous cent and a half a day. In the meantime his wife and children may be starving on the streets outside; he is powerless to help them, and can write only one letter a month. In other words, as a prisoner once said to me bitterly, "At just the time we need our friends the most, they are taken away from us. We must write our one letter a month to a wife, a mother, or some member of the family having special claim. Our friends do not hear from us; they think we are hard and do not care—we are criminals; so they drop us and we are forgotten." [7]

All this Landry explains or suggests; and as we grow confidential he tells me quite frankly of his own troubles and how he comes to be here; the mistakes he had made, his keen desire and strong intention to do better when he goes out and to make good. "My father has stuck by me," he says; "and now I intend to stick by him."

After about half an hour spent in the cells, from eight to eight-thirty, we are off to work. Again the keys are turned in the locks, again the clicking of the levers, again the hurried march along the gallery, again my heavy shoes clump down the iron stairs, again we form in the sunny doorway, again we march down the yard to the basket shop.

As we break ranks my partner, Murphy, comes forward with a cheerful smile. "Well, Mr. Brown, how do you feel to-day?"

"Fine," I respond briefly, and we step to our working table.

"How did you sleep?"

---

[7] Jack Murphy gives me the following information: When a new man arrives in prison and is assigned to a shop the waiter or captain puts his name on a requisition letter list. If this inmate's surname begins with A, he gets his monthly letter on the first Sunday of each month; if his name begins with some other letter, he gets his monthly letter on some other Sunday. If, upon A's arrival, his Sunday has just passed, he has to wait until the first Sunday of the next month comes around; unless some one puts him wise on how to write to the warden for an extra or special letter.

"Not very well; I kept waking up all night."

"Well, don't worry. It's always like that the first night; you'll sleep better to-night."

And with this comforting assurance we hang up our coats and caps and start to work.

The convict instructor, Stuhlmiller, comes to our table. "Well, Brown, how did you like bucket duty?"

"Oh, I've had to do worse things than that," I reply. "I don't know that I should select that particular job from preference; but somebody has to do the cleaning up. That's the reason I was once mayor of Auburn."

The other two are greatly amused at this view of official position; and so we start pleasantly with our basket-making.

Before the morning has far advanced the Captain comes over to me and in a low voice asks would I like to be sent out with a gang to help move some coal. I haven't the least idea what is involved, but I'm keen for anything. I am here to learn all I can. So I answer briefly, "Sure," and he returns to his desk. Presently I hear the name of Brown called out with those of Murphy and eight others. Murphy says, "Come on, Brown, we'll get some fresh air!" I start at once for the door, but Murphy pulls me back; we have to be lined up, counted, ten of us, and duly delivered to another officer who takes us in charge.

There are two heavy cars of coal, it seems, to be moved up grade to the coal pile; and as the prison possesses no dummy or yard engine, this has to be done by hand labor. It seems singularly unintelligent to have things so arranged; but for the present it is all the better for me, as it serves well for exercise. A block and tackle is rigged up and we have repeated tugs of war, during which I get my hands very grimy and receive a number of friendly admonitions not to work too hard. There is also the offer on the part of a pleasant young negro to lend his leather mittens.

"Thank you," I say, "but I think you need them more than I do." (It was stupid of me not to give him the satisfaction of doing this slight service.)

The men on the coal gang, in view of their heavy and disagreeable work, are allowed to talk, it seems; and they certainly make good use of this privilege. There were several negroes among the lot, and they kept us all in roars of laughter. In fact it was as cheery and jolly a lot of fellows as one could find, joking about their work, and about their breakfast, and joshing each other in the best of tempers. While we were waiting to get things arranged for the second car, one of the men who works in our shop good naturedly disposed of much of his week's allowance of chewing tobacco to the crowd.

During all these proceedings I stick pretty close to Murphy, both that I may make no mistakes, and because I am already getting to have a great liking for my sturdy partner. Yesterday I was on my guard with him and I think he was quietly sizing me up; but to-day there is an absence of restraint and a pleasant feeling of comradeship growing up between us, which is not lessened by the discovery that we both like fresh air and exercise. Poor fellow! he gets little enough of either. The forty minutes spent in the vigorous tugs of war with the coal cars start an agreeable glow of health and spirits in both of us.

After the coal job is finished I am for going back at once to the shop, which is close at hand, but Murphy halts me again. "Hold on, Brown, we can't go back just yet." It seems that we must again line up and be counted; then we are escorted by the officer temporarily in charge of us back into the shop, where we are once more counted before we return to our regular places.

In order to make up for lost time Murphy and I work steadily on our basket bottoms; he suggesting that we each watch the other's work, to see whether we are keeping the sides even. A mistake is easier to notice across the table than in your own work closer at hand. My fault seems to be to pull the withes too tight, making the sides somewhat concave; while Murphy has just the opposite fault— he makes his sides too convex. So I watch his work and he watches mine, and all things go on very agreeably.

At one stage in the morning's proceedings I forget where I am, for the moment, and begin to whistle; but a swift and warning look from Murphy startles me into silence.

"Look out," he warns me, "whistling's not allowed. You'll get punished if you ain't careful."

"Is a whistling prisoner worse than a whistling girl?" I ask; but I see that my partner is not acquainted with the proverb, so I repeat it to him:

> "Whistling girls, like crowing hens,
> Always come to some bad ends."

He is much amused at this sentiment, despite its imperfect rhyme, and asks me to repeat it so that he can learn it.

As we are working busily away, I perceive a sudden commotion over at the western end of the shop. One of the poor old prisoners, those mournful wrecks of humanity of which our

43

company has its full share, has fainted, and lies cold and white on the stone floor. It is pleasant to see how tenderly those about him go to his help, raise the poor old fellow, seat him in one of the rough chairs—the best the shop affords—and bathe his forehead with cold water. It is also pleasant to hear the words of sympathy which are passed along from one to another.

In due time a litter is brought; the pitiful fragment of humanity is placed gently upon it, and is carried out of the shop into which he will probably never return. The look on his face is one not easy to forget, in its white stare of patient suffering. It seemed to typify long years of stolid endurance until the worn-out old frame had simply crumbled under the accumulated load.

There may be another lonely deathbed in the hospital to-night. No wife or child, no friend of any sort to smooth the pillow or to close the eyes. Alas, the pity of it!

But the sight is evidently no new one to my comrades. A few minutes only and the shadow has passed. There is even apparent an air of anxiety lest we dwell too much on the mournful episode. It will not do to think of death here; anything—anything but that!

It must be at about half-past eleven that a certain air of restlessness pervading the shop shows that dinner time is approaching. Murphy goes for his soap and towel. "Come on, Brown, and wash up."

"I'm sorry, I forgot and left my soap and towel in my cell."

"Well, never mind, come and use mine."

So, raising my hand for the Captain's permission to leave my place, I join Murphy at the sink, and again we use his soap and towel in common. My partner's treatment of me is certainly very satisfactory; there is just enough of an air of protection suitable for a man who knows the ropes to show toward his partner who does not, combined with an open-hearted deference to an older man of wider experience that somehow is extraordinarily pleasant.

Before going back to the cell-house we march first to the place where we left the buckets this morning before breakfast. Each man secures his own bucket, which is marked with the number of his cell; then we go swinging up the yard, break ranks at the side door of the north wing, up the stairs, traverse the long gallery, and so to my cell around the corner. It begins to have a certain homelike association; but I do dislike having to close the grated door and lock myself in every time.

The gallery boy has been most attentive. I find a rack for my towels and a mirror added to the cell equipment; also he has promised me a better electric light bulb. There are two gallery boys,

I find; one is George, the other is Joe. George is Captain Lamb's trusty, and serves in the shop as well as the gallery. He has been the one who has added my new furnishings. Joe I see only when I am in my cell; and I do not know where he works. He brings me water and has been most genial.

There seems to be about half an hour at noon between the shop and the mess-hall. As soon as I am back in my cell I remove my cap and coat and "slick up" for dinner. Then I chat with any of the trusties that happen to drift along to my cell. One of them brings me a book which a prisoner on our gallery is sending to me. It is Victor Hugo's "Ninety-Three." Opening it I find a note. The writer begins by saying that he had found the book interesting and hoped I would, and then adds, "Some of the guards laughed at you when you passed this morning. I know it is a hard proposition you are up against; but say, stick it out! I only wish I could help you, and I am voicing the sentiments of all the boys who work in the school."

Generous in him to run the risk of punishment in order to send me this word of encouragement.

We march to dinner in the same order as at breakfast, and I find myself again next to the blue-shirted Landry. I like his looks and his personality. It is curious how one can get an effect of that, even under the rigid and unnatural demeanor which the discipline engenders. There is a dapper little chap who leads the right line of our company to whose back I have taken a great liking; some day I hope to get acquainted with his face.

Our dinner is mutton stew, which is really good. I had been told at the shop in the morning what the bill of fare would be; for as one week's dietary is exactly the same as all other weeks, you can calculate with accuracy upon every meal. I eat my dinner with peculiar relish after our morning struggle with the coal car.

Arrived back at the cell, Joe, the other gallery boy, stops to chat, after he has dispensed water along the tier. "Say, Brown," he begins, "do you know after the talk you give us up in chapel on Sunday there was some of us didn't believe you really meant to come down and live with us. Then they thought if you did come you'd manage to get up to the Warden's quarters for supper and a bed. But, say, when the boys see you marchin' down with your bucket this mornin'—they knew you meant business!"

Then the youngster puts his face up close to the bars, squints through them admiringly, looks me all up and down from head to foot, and breaks out with: "Gee! You're a dead game sport!"

On the whole I think that's by far the finest compliment I ever had in my life.

CHAPTER VII
TUESDAY AFTERNOON AND EVENING

In my cell, Tuesday evening, September 30.

Laying aside my journal this noon, I don my coat and cap and stand ready at the cell door. The Captain passes by, unlocking the levers; then repasses, pushing them down, and I am ready to fall in line as usual; but one of the gray figures stops suddenly and whispers to me, "Your cup! You've forgotten your cup!" So I create a momentary halt and confusion in the gallery as I dash back into the cell to get my tin cup and out again, leaving it on the shelf at the entrance. We traverse the gallery, descend the iron stairs, line up at the door, march first slowly then rapidly down the yard, through the sewage disposal building to the bucket stands; and so to the basket-shop again.

"Well, Brown, how did you enjoy your dinner, good?" This question is my partner's afternoon greeting.

"Good! I should say it was! I'd like to tackle another car of coal this afternoon to give me such an appetite. No, on second thoughts, not this afternoon—to-morrow morning. I don't think I'd better get up much of an appetite with nothing but bread and water ahead of me."

Murphy laughs. "Well, we've got two bottoms each to do this afternoon, to make up for our exercise this morning; so we must hustle up and get 'em done."

So we both start basket-making; he joking at my efforts to keep up with him, and I, in a futile attempt to do so, "working like a race-horse," as he expresses it. With pleasant chat the time passes quickly. The strangeness of my situation is beginning to wear away; and the men are getting over their aloofness as they see that, in Joe's words, I mean business; and also see how well I get along with my partner and my boss. The latter, the smiling Stuhlmiller, drops round to our table frequently; makes valuable and friendly criticism and suggestion as to my work, by which I try to profit; and incidentally tells many things which both directly and indirectly throw valuable light upon the life here. As a workman I must pay my tribute of admiration to Stuhlmiller; his small, delicate hands with strong, pliable fingers are made for craftsmanship. It gives positive delight to see him take hold of the weaving, to show me or someone else how it should be done. There are the elements of the

46

real artist of some sort in that chap. What a pity to have these rare qualities wasted in prison!

In the course of the afternoon a party of visitors is shown through the shop by the Warden in person. It is only this evening that I have learned all the facts of this incident, as I was so busy working that I never noticed the party at all; although they walked by, only a few feet away, passing directly between me and the keeper. This is the story as I get it first hand, from the Warden himself.

It seems that some newspaper men from New York were in town to-day and were most anxious to see Tom Brown at work. The strict order that everything at the prison was to go on exactly as usual forbade their interviewing me, or even having me pointed out; but there was nothing to prevent their being shown over the prison in the ordinary way. The Warden, who had returned from Albany, thinking he would like to take the opportunity of himself seeing his "new boarder" at work, offered to conduct them. So down through the yard they all came and in due course reached the basket-shop.

"This is the place where Tom Brown is working," remarked the Warden; "but, gentlemen, please remember you are not to speak to him or even seem to give him special notice."

So they entered the shop and leisurely made their way through; the Warden exchanging a word or two with the Captain as he went by, and all of them looking curiously at the various basket-makers within sight.

After they had passed out of the shop at the farther end, one of the visitors said,

"But, Warden, I didn't see him."

"Neither did we," chimed in the rest.

"Well, gentlemen," laughed the Warden, "this is certainly one on me; for I looked everywhere and I couldn't find him myself."

It was true; the whole party had passed within twenty feet of me, and not one of them—not even my intimate friend—had recognized me.

"But I'm very sure he's there," continued the Warden; "at any rate I can verify it at my office."

So they returned to the main building and found out, sure enough, that Thomas Brown was duly registered in the basket-shop.

Two of the visitors insisted upon returning; they had known me very well by sight and were sure they could find me out. So back they came to the shop, and this time I noticed them.

"I wonder who those guys are, rubbering around?" is my remark to Murphy, speaking in the vernacular, as we are

47

working away. I was taking good care not to stare hard at them in my turn.

"They're not looking at you, anyhow," is Murphy's report. I steal another glance and catch an intent, searching look from one of the visitors. I am just finishing off a basket bottom and have on eyeglasses of unusual shape—rather too fine for Tom Brown. I fear that the visitor may have spotted these. However, I return his stare insolently, with as much of the air of an old timer as I can muster on the spur of the moment. At the same instant I whisper some joke over to Murphy that makes him smile; and the guy moves on, staring at others of my shopmates in their turn.

"I guess he was after me, all right," I remark to my partner, "and I'm afraid these infernal specs may have given me away."

As a matter of fact the two visitors returned from the basket-shop again disappointed. One of them thought he had seen Tom Brown, but wasn't quite sure. My identity seems to be sufficiently merged—so far as outsiders are concerned.

Toward the close of the afternoon my talk with my partner becomes more serious. In spite of the rules, newspapers seem to circulate here and are precious in proportion to their rarity. Some one hands a paper to Murphy, who passes it over to me; and I, after glancing over it, hand it back to him to be returned. The editor of this particular sheet, in commenting upon my adventure, expressed doubt as to the possibility of "the amateur convict" being able to get hold of the real life of the prison. This view makes me smile, under the circumstances, and I ask Murphy what he thinks about it. His reply is that there is no doubt of my being able to get all I want, and getting it straight.

"Well, I want to know all there is," I lightly rejoin, "and I'm thinking of breaking the rules in some way before I get out of here, so as to be sent down to the punishment cells."

A look of genuine concern comes over my partner's face, and his voice sinks to an awestruck whisper. "Do you mean the jail?" he asks.

"Yes," I answer; "I want to learn everything possible about this place, so I think I may as well spend at least one night in jail."

"Well, you'd better be careful." My partner speaks slowly and impressively. There can be no doubt of his sincerity; a glance at his earnest, troubled face settles that. "I went down to that place once," he continues; "and I want to tell you—after eight hours of it I just caved right in! I told them that they could do anything they liked with me."

"Was it so very bad?" I ask.

"Well, my advice to you is to give it a wide berth," is his evasive answer. Then there is silence between us for a moment, and when he begins again it is evident that his thoughts have turned into a still more serious channel. "Yes, you can learn a great deal, but let me tell you this, Brown: no one can realize what this place really is like, until—until—well, until there is someone he cares about who is sick and he can't get away." There is a tremor in his voice. Poor fellow! The Chaplain told me last night that Murphy had recently lost his mother and felt her death very deeply.

This talk occurs at the end of the day's work when we are waiting for the Captain's signal of return, and Murphy is sitting on the edge of the table talking quietly, turning his head away from the Captain and toward me as I stand on my regular side of the table.

I place a hand on my partner's broad shoulder. "Yes," I say, "it must indeed be terrible in such a case."

"Oh, nobody can know how bad it is," he goes on, my evident sympathy opening up the depths. "My mother was sick in the hospital, very sick, and I knew that she was going to die; and I—and I couldn't get to her. Oh God! if they could only have let me go! I'd have come back! I'd have come back. Honest I would. And now— and now——"

"Yes," I say, "I understand. And I know myself what it means. It's something we never get over—in prison or out."

For a moment I fear that he is going to break down; but he is strong and schooled in self-repression, and quickly regains control of himself. To give him time I tell him something of my own experience; and he grasps my hand fervently. Whatever may come out of my prison experiment, I have made at least one warm friend in Jack Murphy. The barriers are down between us two at least. Death, for all its cruelty, is after all the one great unifying force; it forges the one great bond of human brotherhood.

As I have said, this last talk takes place toward the end of the afternoon. Before it occurred Jack had said, "Now it's my turn to sweep up to-night." And he proceeded to do it, while I took a bit of exercise, walking up and down the short space permitted by the rules—about ten steps each way across and back.

The order comes to fall in. "Well, good night, Brown!" "Good night, Jack!" and off we go; first back to the bucket stands, for the benefit of those who did their housecleaning this afternoon instead of this morning. Then we march up through the yard to the main building, where, with the others, I snatch my slice of bread, mount the iron stairs, traverse the gallery, and lock myself in my cell for the night.

Captain Lamb comes to bid me good-bye. He is off on his vacation to-morrow and his place is to be filled temporarily by one of the night officers. I am sorry to have him go as I have taken a liking to him and wanted to discuss with him further his views on the Prison Problem. However, I shall be interested to find out how we get along with his successor.

The armchair, which George has secured for me in place of the stool, is unfortunately much too large for the cell. When my shelf table is hooked up there is not room enough for the chair to be placed anywhere conveniently. When I sit back in it my head bumps against the locker; and how I'm going to manage when the bed is let down I don't know. The chair is not my only acquisition; when I came in to-night I found three tempting apples on the shelf above my door. I suspect my friend in the blue shirt, who asked me this noon if I didn't want an apple, as his Captain had given him some. I shall save them for to-morrow, although I find my bread and water rather tasteless and unsatisfactory to-night.

The evening wears along. I do not know now just what time it is, but somewhere between seven and eight. We have had the twenty minutes of music, beginning again with the sweet strains of the Mendelssohn Spring Song, into which the other instruments rudely break. My unknown musician plays other good selections, all with equal skill and feeling, so far as I can tell through the din. At the present moment everything is quiet along the corridors, except the inexplicable clicking or tapping I heard last evening and wondered whether it was telegraphic in character. One of the night officers, who has just paid me a friendly call and chatted at some length, tells me that it is caused by the endeavors of the men in the cells to strike sparks with flint and steel—owing to their monthly supply of matches having given out. As the monthly supply of each man is only one box, I am not surprised at the number of clicks that I hear. A cigarette smoker might easily use up one box in a day—let alone a month. [8]

---

[8] On this point Jack Murphy writes: "We are allowed one box of matches a month. The men split each match into two parts, so as to make this one box last as long as possible. Each box contains 62 matches. After they are split up into two the prisoner has 124 matches. These will last him about 10 days; then he must use his flint and steel. This is the most intelligent thing the convicts are taught, for it teaches them the art of economy, which, if lived up to, will help them to overcome their extravagance when freed." I believe our friend B. intimated that Jack is something of a joker.

It is very curious the difference between last evening and this in my feelings. Then I was so excited that each noise got on my nerves. To-night I am quiet; and I think sleep will come more easily and stay longer. Perhaps I can even slumber through the visits of the watchman with his electric bull's-eye.

At this point I was interrupted by the Warden and Grant, who have just paid me a long call. As I feel even more possessed with the desire to talk than I did last night, I could hardly bear to let them go. They came up to the entrance of my cell very quietly so as not to attract attention, and I was taken almost by surprise when I heard their voices. I had rather expected a visit from the Warden this evening, but knew nothing for certain.

"Well, how are you coming on?" is the first question.

"Fine!"

"How are you feeling?"

"First rate!"

"How do you like your job?"

"Couldn't ask anything better."

"How do the men treat you?"

"As fine a lot of fellows as I was ever thrown with."

The Warden and Grant stifle their laughter.

"Well," I remark, "I suppose it does sound rather funny, but I mean it. I wouldn't ask for any better treatment than I'm getting. The men are certainly acting like gentlemen. They are doing just what I asked of them—treating me exactly like one of themselves; and as for my partner, Murphy, we're the very best of friends. He's a fine fellow. But look here," I continue, "I'm making no kick, and I'm perfectly satisfied where I am; but what was the reason for the change of plan? Why didn't the P. K. put me where we had decided? When shall I be placed with that tough bunch?"

This time my two visitors cannot control their amusement; they laugh loudly.

"Why," says the Warden, as soon as he can catch his breath, "you are with the tough bunch!"

"Oh, come off! you know what I mean, the Idle Company that I was to be placed with for the first day or two."

"You're with the Idle Company," explains the Warden; "only

Since my week in prison the inmates are allowed to buy a dozen boxes of matches a month. Why they should not always have been allowed to do so is beyond my comprehension.

51

they're not idle any longer, they've been put to work. It is the same one where we planned for you to begin."

I was never more surprised; but in order to turn the joke on them I assume the toughest manner at my disposal and say, "Gee! Did you think I wasn't wise? I was only kiddin' youse guys! But take this from me—straight. If we're the toughest bunch in this stir the other guys must be skypilots, all right!"

"Well, he seems to be getting some of the lingo down pretty fine," is Grant's quiet comment; and then we turn seriously to the events of the day, to my health and other matters. The Warden describes his visit to the shop with the newspaper men, and the failure of all concerned, including himself, to recognize me.

I tell him that it is quite evident that the prison atmosphere has been successful in disguising my individuality, at least so far as appearance is concerned. Then, after some more serious talk, we reach an agreement of opinion that I am probably getting as much experience as possible where I am now working; and so it would be better to continue in the basket-shop for the present. The Warden makes me a promise to come again to-morrow evening, and they take their departure. I wish they'd come back, I haven't talked half enough.

The Warden told me that one of the convicts who works in his household quarters locks in (to use the prison expression denoting temporary residence) next to me—Number 14 on this tier; and that he had felt rather hurt that I did not answer his taps. It seems that after finishing his evening's work he gets back to his cell at ten o'clock, and that he tapped me a greeting last night. That was just about the time I fell asleep. I remember getting the impression in a vague way of some noises on the gallery near by, just as I was dropping off; that must have been the night officer letting him into his cell. To-night I shall stay awake and answer his message.

So the company I am in is the one I have been dreading, is it? "The toughest bunch of fellows in the prison"—Murphy and Stuhlmiller and "Blackie," the good-natured fellow who gave away his tobacco and brings us the material for our baskets; and the other pleasant men whose acquaintance I have been making these last two days in the shop. It is incredible, inconceivable. What can be the explanation of it all?

Is it possible that I am being made the victim of a clever system of deception? This is naturally my first thought. I can well imagine that Jack Murphy enjoys the novel sensation of having as his partner a man who is for the moment an object of peculiar interest to this community, that is simply human nature. No doubt

Harley Stuhlmiller enjoys giving directions to the member of a state commission, that again is human nature. But that these men could assume virtues which they have not, and carry out a wholesale system of deceit—that is not possible. I have been on my guard every moment I have been here, and I have observed some few attempts to get into my good graces, with a possible expectation of future benefits; but on the other hand there has been a remarkable and most successful effort to carry out my request—to treat me as plain Tom Brown.

No, that explanation doesn't explain; the truth must lie in another direction. And here is my idea. I am not seeing the worse side of these men because there is no occasion for them to show me their worse side; but I have no intention of overlooking or denying that side. They wouldn't be in prison if they did not have it. But, although they may form the toughest bunch in prison, they evidently have their better side also, and is that not just as real as the worse side? And is it not the better side that is the more important for us to consider? Important—whether we approach the matter from the side of philanthropy or from that of political economy. In either case we must consider it important that men should not leave prison in such condition, mental, moral or physical, that they will almost certainly commit more crimes and be returned to prison.

To which side, the better or the worse, does the Prison System now appeal? Which does it encourage and develop? These are pretty vital questions.

At any rate it seems to me to have been great good luck that I was placed in the basket-shop where I should associate with just these men; for if these fellows are really among the more difficult cases in the prison, then I think——

Wednesday morning, October 1.

At that interesting moment, while still writing my journal, the lights suddenly went out on me; so I am finishing this next morning. The Warden and Grant arrived soon after eight and must have stayed longer than I thought; and somehow I seem to have missed the warning bell. I had not begun to prepare for bed, when suddenly I was left in darkness. I had to get my writing materials into the locker and make my evening toilet the best way I could, with the help of the dim light from the corridor coming through the grated door. There was one good thing about it, however; I was too busy for a while to notice the blackness of the bars which had given me such a shock the night before. It did not take so very long to make my preparations, for the state of New York allows its boarders neither night shirts nor pajamas. We have to sleep in the underclothes in which we have worked all day. An arrangement which strikes one as being almost more medieval than the sewage disposal system.

On Monday night, according to Jack Murphy, the men in my corridor all waited to hear if I had the usual difficulties with my bed; and as some other fellow's bed went down with him during the evening they thought they had the laugh on me. This Tuesday night they certainly had. That infernal armchair could not be placed where it did not catch the edge of the bed when I let it down, so as to leave one leg dangling loose, as only one could touch the floor at a time. In the course of my struggles with the bed, the whole miserable contrivance came off the hooks and fell down with a metallic rattle and bang that could be heard all over the corridor. Then came snickers from various distances, and my frantic effort to straighten things out only made more noise than ever. Bursts of smothered laughter came through the bars; and I laughed, myself, until I was almost in hysterics. Finally I got the bed hitched on to the back hooks, folded it up against the wall and started all over again. I began by putting the chair on its back as far away from the bed as possible, which wasn't very far, and this time I just managed to get the legs of the bed to the floor. After that it was short work to get ready for the night.

I have not yet described my bed covering. I have one double and one single blanket and a thin blanket sheet—no cotton or linen of any sort. I do not need, in this weather, more than one of the three blankets; but if I were to be here long I know I should like some cotton bedclothes and pillow cases. These can be secured, apparently, only by buying them, and many prisoners have not the money to buy them. It seems as if the State should furnish them to all prisoners; certainly the present arrangement leaves much to be desired from a sanitary point of view.

Having thus at last got into bed, I found myself not so sleepy as when I started; moreover, now that I was in bed, that black grating began again to have its nervous effect upon me. If I thought it would be any better I should turn, facing the other way; but that would bring my head so close to the grating that anyone from outside could poke me with his fingers. Moreover, it wouldn't help matters, for as long as I know that grating is there I might as well look at it; I should certainly feel it even worse if I turned my back.

I heard the nine-fifty train drawing into the station. I wondered who, if any, of my friends were boarding the train for

New York. How often have I done so without ever thinking of the poor fellows over here, lying restless in their cells and marking the time by the arrival and departure of trains. After a suitable interval I heard the train draw away. Then I knew that in a few moments my neighbor from the Warden's rooms would be down.

Soon I heard the opening and closing of a distant door, then stealthy footfalls along the corridor, the faint sound of a lock, and I saw the long iron bar slowly and noiselessly raise itself from the top of the cell opening. Then more stealthy footfalls, the sound of the great key turning in a lock close at hand, the click of a lever, and a few faint sounds through the wall at my right. Then the lever clicked again as the door closed, the key turned in the lock, soft footfalls died away along the gallery, the long bar dropped down, and all was so quiet for a moment that it seemed as if the very building were holding its breath.

Then through the wall I heard the very faintest possible sound: tap-ta-tap-tap; tap-ta-tap-tap. Then silence. It was so faint that if I had not been waiting for some sound I might not have heard it at all. Tap-ta-tap-tap. It said quite plainly, "How do you do?" I stretched out my left hand to the wall on my right and with my ring gave an answering signal: Tap-tap; tap-tap; tap-tap; which was the nearest I could come to, "All right; all right." Then I waited to see if I was answered; and sure enough in a few seconds the answer came.

After some moments, during which I presume my unseen friend was preparing for bed, I heard again a different sound; rap-rap, rap-rap, rap-rap. It said as plain as possible, "Good-night, good-night." So I returned it in the same way. Then turning over in my narrow bed I fell asleep, and although my sleep was neither deep nor continuous it was much better than the night before.

CHAPTER VIII
WEDNESDAY MORNING AND AFTERNOON

In my cell, Wednesday evening, October 2.

Looking out of the upper windows in the outer wall, from the door of my cell, I can see that the morning is cloudy and threatening. It is also warmer; up to now it has been clear and cool.

I feel in good condition after a very fair night, and rise soon after hearing the six o'clock westbound train and the factory whistles. This gives me ample time to wash, dress, and get completely ready for the day.

The new acting Captain starts in this morning—Captain Kane. He is a handsome, neat and soldierly appearing officer, with cold blue eyes and a forceful quiet manner. Promptly on time he unlocks the levers, and George, the trusty, follows close after, pushing them down. Around the corner there is a slight delay, as the long bar on that tier seems to be somewhat out of order and will not rise far enough to allow the doors of the cells to swing open. I'm glad I'm not in one of those cells or I should be afraid of being shut in for the day. The Captain soon gets the bar raised, however, and the usual routine happens; walking along the gallery with our heavy buckets, descending the iron stairs, waiting in the passage at the door of the north wing, and marching down the yard to the sewage disposal building. Then the rapid cleaning of the buckets, leaving them to be aired and disinfected at the stands; and the march back to our cells. It is, as I supposed, a gray, cloudy day, with rain likely to come. If it does, there is no change of clothing whatever in my cell, and no way of getting one that I know of; so I hope it will not rain. But what do these poor fellows do after marching through the yard in a real drenching shower? Work until they're dry, I suppose, if they get wet on the way to the shop; or go to bed in their cells if they get wet on the way back. This holds out to me a cheerful prospect of wet clothes all day and fourteen hours in bed in case it rains hard; for the distance from the cell block to the basket-shop would be a long walk in the rain.

What an admirable system! Excellently calculated, I should imagine, to produce the largest possible crop of pneumonia in the shortest possible space of time.

Upon my return to the cell I do my morning sweeping. I do not know where all the dust comes from, as no one else uses the cell, and I can't see where I collect any; but dusty it is every morning.

Then I have a call from Dickinson, the Chaplain's assistant. The poor fellow has a letter from the man who had promised him work, saying that the factory is running slack and there is no knowing how soon his job will be ready for him. He had counted on Saturday being his day of release, his wife was coming to meet him, and all his plans were made for a joyful family reunion. Now it must all go by the board. It is a heart-breaking disappointment, but he bears up bravely.

As it happens I may be able to help him. At any rate I promise to write a letter to his proposed employer. The poor fellow grasps at this slight comfort and expresses his gratitude most fervently. Then I turn my attention to breakfast.

Wednesday's breakfast consists of hash, with the usual accompaniments of boot-leg and punk. I was told in the shop yesterday what to expect. The smell of the mess-room is beginning to be unpleasant, perhaps owing to the change in temperature. If so, what it must be on a moist warm day in summer, or on a wet day in winter when the steam is turned on, I hate to think.

The hash is not so good as yesterday's porridge. Moreover it is rendered distinctly less appetizing by the amount of bone and gristle which I find chopped up in it. I hope I am not unduly fastidious in such matters, and an occasional inedible morsel I should not criticize; but an average of two or three pieces of bone and gristle to a mouthful seems to me excessive.

Back in my cell I write my promised letter on behalf of Dickinson; but the minutes before shop time pass so quickly that when the lever is pressed down I am not ready, and so have to make a grab for my coat and cap and fall in toward the end of the line on the gallery. During the halt at the door, however, I regain my place— third in line on the left. The rain has come, but, fortunately, it is little more than a mist. It gives me a chance, however, to venture a mild pleasantry. When the Captain is out of hearing I whisper, with as English an accent as possible, "Oh, dear me! Where did I leave my umber-rella?" a remark which causes unseemly snickers from those within hearing. The joke is quite in character, as those I hear turn largely on the various hardships and privations of prison life; although the one huge, massive, gigantic joke, which is always fresh and pointed, is the current rate of payment for a prisoner's work— one cent and a half a day. Before this monumental and gorgeous piece of humor all other jokes seem flat and pointless.

On the march down the yard to the shop we pass the Warden. He lets us go by without any sign of recognition, which gives me another chance to get a laugh from my comrades. I whisper, "So that is the way my old friends treat me!" Apparently the prisoners can appreciate a joke better than an official; I am still a bit resentful at the way that excessively bored Bertillon clerk received my attempt at humor.

Arrived at the shop I go directly to my bench, and turning around am greeted by the cheery face of my partner. He comes up behind me, for he marches somewhere in the rear. "Well, Brown, how did you get by last night?"

"Better, thank you, Jack!"

57

"Well, of course you will find it hard for the first week or two, but after that you will be O. K." By which it will be seen that my partner likes a joke as well as the next man. Then as we hang up our caps and coats and get ready for work he continues, "A new man always does find it hard to sleep when he is thinking of a wife or mother or someone else at home; but as soon as the mist clears away he begins to see and think more clearly."

I am about to answer when a warning whisper, "Look out! Here comes the screw!" tells me that our new Captain is approaching.

"How many bottoms do you two men make a day?" asks that officer.

I look at Murphy and he promptly answers, "Five."

"Then continue making five for a day's work, just as you were doing under your regular officer," says the Captain; and moves on to the next pair of men. Our new officer evidently does not propose to have the work slack off during his management of the shop.

My other shopmates have greeted me warmly, and presently I have pleasant conversations with some of them. To-day for the first time the ice is thoroughly broken, and I am quite made one of them. It happens in this way.

As we are working away, Jack and I, trying to accomplish our morning's task with very stiff material to work with, the P. K. shows up. He has come, I suppose, to see how the new Captain is getting on with the toughest bunch of fellows in the prison. After he has conversed awhile with the Captain he walks slowly over to where we are working and remarks, apparently addressing the world in general, "Don't you feel the draught from that door?"

As he has not spoken to anyone in particular, I look at Jack and wait for him or somebody else to answer; but Jack is bending over his work and no one seems inclined to say anything.

"Thank you, sir," I begin politely; "as far as I am concerned I don't mind it, for I like fresh air. It doesn't trouble me any."

"Well now," says the portly and dignified dispenser of law and order, "I don't want you men to catch cold. I think you'd better have that door shut and perhaps the windows farther open. I'll just speak to the Captain about it. You mustn't work in a draught if you feel it too much."

As the P. K. steps back to the Captain I glance over at Murphy and catch an answering gleam in his eye. "It's all right, Jack," I remark, in a cautious undertone, "I'm wise."

He grins. "Well, did you ever see anything so raw as that?"

I chuckle, and glance sarcastically over toward our highly

respected officers. Jack continues, "Does he think he can put that over on us?"

"Not this time," is my reply; and when the Captain, upon the P. K.'s departure, comes over to shut the door I tell him that if he doesn't mind we should prefer to have it left open, to which suggestion he kindly yields. It is a large double door and gives light as well as fresh air to all our part of the shop.

This little episode has not gone unnoticed by the rest of the men; I almost instantly feel that I have risen several pegs in the esteem of my comrades. Several of them who have hitherto held aloof come over for an introduction to Tom Brown. If I am on the side of the convicts against the officers, in short if I am "ag'in the government," I must be all right. I am perfectly conscious of the barriers giving way. Of course the game I am playing has its dangers, but I believe it is the wise one. If I am really to gain these men's confidence, I must be on the convicts' side and act the part completely. I must look at matters from the convicts' point of view; and scorn of all forms of hypocrisy and double dealing on the part of those in authority as well as good faith with your pals seems to be the platform upon which all the best men stand. And these are mighty fine qualities outside prison; why then are they not equally fine inside? Are not truth and courage and devotion to be welcomed wherever found? And are not falsehood and hypocrisy always hateful? A certain man who is serving time here, although innocent of the crime for which he was sent, because he could not escape conviction without implicating two of his friends is a type. "But then," he once explained to me, "you see, I had done a good many things for which I had not served time. And our code of ethics is based upon the rule that you must never squeal on a pal." It was the same man who, when he once started to complain of the injustice of some term he had served and I had said, "Yes, but you must consider the other side of it," broke into a smile and answered:

"You are entirely right. I've calculated that I still owe the state of New York two or three hundred years."

But all that is another story.

Before the morning is over George, the trusty, comes along saying: "Shave, Jack?" "Yes." "Shave, Brown?" "No, thank you."

So my partner goes under George's hands for his semiweekly barbering, and in due time reappears, looking his best. If anyone should ask me how good is Jack's best, I should have to answer that I have not the least idea. By this time I am becoming so attached to my open-hearted, whole-souled partner that I can only look at him with the eyes of affectionate and indiscriminating friendship.

While Jack is getting shaved I work on steadily, chatting with Stuhlmiller, "Blackie," whose name I find is Laflam, and Jack Bell, who marches second in line on the right, and who has a pleasant voice and seems like an exceptionally intelligent fellow.

We return to the cell house at the usual time; and fortunately the rain has ceased, so I do not have the experience of a wet day—an experience I am quite willing to forego.

At dinner we have pork and beans, the beans not at all bad. We also have tea instead of coffee. I can make out but very little difference in these two beverages. I should say they must both be prepared in some such apparatus as is described by the boy in "Mugby Junction": "A metallic object that's at times the tea-urn and at times the soup-tureen, according to the nature of the last twang imparted to its contents which are the same groundwork."

After dinner I have a long talk with Roger Landry. He grows confidential, telling much about himself—completing the story, part of which he gave me yesterday. It interests me greatly. And it is just this vital human element that is making my experiment so much more absorbing than I had expected.

At the usual time we march back to the shop, where I have two new experiences.

The first is a glimpse of the school. I am working away steadily with Jack when an officer suddenly appears at my elbow. "Is this Thomas Brown?"

"Yes, sir."

"The Professor wants to see you at the school."

Meekly putting on my cap and coat, I follow the keeper out of the shop. At least I prepare to follow—I wait for him to lead the way, but he motions me to go ahead of him. Then I realize that an officer escorting a convict always walks just behind, where he can keep a watchful eye on every move of his charge.

The school is only a few steps away, in fact in the second story of the very building of which our shop occupies the ground floor. I ascend the stairs, and passing through a hall find myself in the principal's office. Here I am told to wait until the Professor is at leisure. I wait a long time. When he arrives he gives me a single sheet of paper, and tells me to write a composition on the subject of My Education.

I sit down and quickly fill two pages with a succinct account of my stay at different institutions of learning, ending with my graduation from the university. Then I simply add that, while this has been the end of my schooling, I hope my education is still going on.

The Professor having left the room again while I am writing, I have another considerable wait. The school appears to be much larger and more important than when I saw it last, some years ago. I should like to see more of it. After a while the Professor returns and reads over my paper. His only comment is one regarding my university degree. The Chaplain has already told me that there are twenty college graduates confined in prison here, but I am pleased to have the Professor add the information that I am the only Harvard graduate in the institution. I repress the inevitable impulse to say, "I suppose the others come from Yale," and simply express gratification at what the Professor has told me. I have already decided to reserve all jokes for my comrades.

"That is all, Brown."

"Thank you, sir."

I cannot even be trusted to go down one flight of stairs and walk not more than thirty steps to the door of the basket-shop; so another wait is necessary until the keeper who brought me up is ready to take me back. He in time reappears and returns me, like a large and animated package, to Captain Kane. I appear to have satisfied the authorities with my mental equipment.

My second new experience to-day is the bath. The order to fall in comes soon after my return from the school. We are lined up and counted—35 of us—each man with his towel, soap and bundle of clean clothes. My fresh apparel appeared yesterday in the shop and George kindly took care of it for me until to-day. We march in due order to a large bathhouse where are rows of shower baths with small anterooms for dressing, arranged about three sides of a large, oblong room with a raised promenade for the officers down the middle. I am for plunging at once into my section, heedless of the careful instructions Jack has given me, but one of my companions stops me, and I wait like the others with my back to the door until we have all been counted and placed. Then the word is given, and I enter. Here is a very small space where I undress, handing the shirt, socks, and underclothes I take off to an attendant who sticks his hand under the door to get them. Then I enjoy a good warm shower for a few moments, but cut it short, having been warned that I must not waste any time. The drying and dressing are rather harder than the disrobing in such confined quarters, but are successfully accomplished, and I am among the first to emerge and take up my station outside, with my back to the door again. The officer, who has been walking up and down his elevated perch, keeping close watch of our heads while we bathed, counts us all carefully when the space in front of every man's door is occupied. We then are marched back to the shop, are again counted, and then disperse to our work.

But the excitements of the day are not yet over. As Jack and I are working hard to make up for lost time, I suddenly see over to the left, out of the corner of my eye, a familiar figure. It is my nephew. He is followed by another familiar figure and another and another. The Warden is showing over the prison a party of visitors, among them several of my intimate friends.

I fear that the remark with which I explode will not bear repetition.

"What's the matter?" says Jack, looking up from his work.

"Nothing," I reply, "it's only my nephew, confound him, and some other rubbernecks. For Heaven's sake, Jack, work away as usual and don't attract any attention if we can help it."

My eyeglasses are in my pocket; and fearing that my ring may catch the light I hastily drop it also into another pocket. Then I put on my cap and continue my work as naturally as possible, without looking up.

Certainly, so far as appearances go, the prison system is a success in my case. In arithmetic, as I recall it, we used to seek for the greatest common denominator and the least common multiple; but in prison the apparent object is to find the least common denominator—the lowest common plane upon which you can treat everyone alike, college graduate and Bowery tough, sick and well, imbecility and intelligence, vice and virtue.

In appearance, as I started to say, I am apparently all that could be desired. Just as happened yesterday, the Warden leads this party through the shop; they are all looking specially for me; they have been spurred on by the failure of the newspaper men yesterday and are one and all determined to find me. Yet they one and all pass within twenty feet, look straight in my direction—and go on their way without recognizing me. I must have the marks of "the Criminal" unusually developed, or else criminals must look a good deal like other folks—barring the uniform. If I had the ordinary theories about prisons and prisoners it might seem rather mortifying that, in spite of every effort, not one of these intimate friends can spot me among the toughest bunch of fellows in the prison.

Certainly something must be wrong somewhere.

This appears to be an afternoon of excitements. Down comes the P. K. again, for what purpose I do not know. The afternoon is cloudy and it is getting somewhat dark and gloomy in the shop. After the P. K. has spoken to the Captain he comes over and tells us fellows that we can quit work if we want to, as it is too dark to see well. He points to the north windows, where a car of lumber on the track outside interferes somewhat with the light in that part of the shop. After he is gone we continue working, as we can see perfectly well; and Jack is still more scornful than he was this morning. He expresses the opinion that this proceeding is even more raw than the former one. "I should like to know how long it is since they was so careful of our eyes, so awful anxious about our health!" is his sarcastic comment.

My answering comment is this, "I dare say, Jack, it's all right; but, so far as I am concerned, they can't come it over me that way."

"Well, I guess not!" is Jack's hearty response.

After we have washed up and just before we separate for the night my partner comes up to me in his engaging way. "Say, would you mind if I called you by your first name?"

"Mind! I should like it; and I wish you would." As a matter of fact I had been intending to ask him to do so.

So now it is "Good night, Tom," "Good night, Jack!" when the time comes to fall in.

As we turn into the yard, I see a group of men gathered about the entrance of the main building. I suspect it to be the same party of rubbernecks the Warden conducted through the shop this afternoon—including my friends. They are evidently waiting for us to march by. As we draw nearer I find that my suspicions are confirmed. I conclude that they failed to discover me in the shop, and so are taking this means of gratifying their curiosity. They are welcome to do so. I look as unconscious as possible; go swinging by the group, eyes front; pick up a slice of bread and regain my cell as usual.

It seems that this time two or three of them, recognizing my walk, spotted me at last. I should think it was about time.

Soon after I am in the cell my friend Joe, the gallery boy, comes along with the hot beverage called tea, which is a little later than usual to-night. He halts at the door.

"Tea, Tommy?"

One of the prisoners has sent me a letter in which he addresses me as "old pal."

I think there is no doubt that the barriers are down now.

CHAPTER IX
WEDNESDAY EVENING

In my cell, later Wednesday evening, October 2.

Upon arriving back here this afternoon, and before sitting down to my usual supper of bread and water, I shave leisurely. In spite of the jar of hot water which George has kindly brought to the cell before I am locked in for the night, my toilet arrangements leave much to be desired. It is true I have shaved at times under greater disadvantages. As, for instance, in camp, when I have had to use the inside of my watch-cover for a mirror. Here in prison I have at least a real mirror, such as it is.

My toilet completed, I make as much of a meal as I can of bread and water. Then I take up my journal to chronicle the events of the day.

The twenty minutes of musical pandemonium come and go, the violinist as usual being the first to begin. Perhaps he may be the fortunate possessor of a watch. Then, also as usual, a silence follows, rendered all the more profound by reason of the previous discord. The cell-house has settled down for the night. Only a few muffled sounds make the stillness more distinctly felt. Then——

Suddenly the unearthly quiet is shattered by a terrifying uproar.

It is too far away to hear at first anything with distinctness; it is all a confused and hideous mass of shouting—a shouting first of a few, then of more, then of many voices. I have never heard anything more dreadful—in the full meaning of the word—full of dread. My heart is thumping like a trip hammer, and the cold shivers run up and down my back.

I jump to the door of the cell, pressing my ear close against the cold iron bars. Then I can distinguish a few words sounding against the background of the confused outcry. "Stop that!" "Leave him alone!" "Damn you, stop that!" Then some dull thuds; I even fancy that I hear something like a groan, along with the continued confused and violent shouting.

What can it be?

While I am perfectly aware that I am not in the least likely to be harmed, I am shivering with something close akin to a chill of actual terror. If anyone near at hand were to give vent to a sudden yell, I feel as if I might easily lose my self-control and shout and bang my door with the rest of them.

The cries continue, accompanied with other noises that I cannot make out. Then my attention is attracted by whispering down at one of the lower windows in the outer wall of the corridor opposite my cell. It is so dark outside that I can see nothing, not even the dim shapes of the whisperers; but apparently there are two of them, and they are looking in and commenting on the disturbance. Their sinister whispering is very unpleasant. I wonder if they can see what is going on. I feel inclined to call out and ask them, but I do not know who they are; and I do know that such an act would be entirely against the rules and liable to provoke severe punishment, and I am not yet ready to be sent to the jail.

The shouts die down. There are a few more vague and uncertain sounds—all the more dreadful for being uncertain; somewhere an iron door clangs! then stillness follows, like that of the grave.

It is useless—I can make nothing of it all; so I sit down again and try to compose my mind to write, but the effort is not very successful. Presently, just after the bell at the City Hall has given its eight o'clock stroke, the Warden appears quietly at the opening of my cell.

"Something has happened," I begin breathlessly, "I don't know what it is, but it ought to be looked into——"

I come to an abrupt stop, for I am suddenly aware of the figure of a man standing in the shadow just behind the Warden.

"Who is that?" I ask, and he steps farther along the gallery, but not where the light from the cell can strike him.

"Only the night officer," answers the Warden.

That is all very well; but why was the night officer lurking in the dark behind the Warden? I decide to ask him a plain, direct question; for he has already heard what is uppermost in my mind.

"Captain," I say, politely, "what was that noise I heard a short while ago?"

The officer, pretending that he has not heard my question, turns to the Warden with some perfectly irrelevant remark, and moves off, along the gallery.

It strikes me as a curious proceeding.

"Warden," I begin again, after waiting until the man must be out of hearing, "I heard shouting off in the corridor somewhere, not very long ago; and I am afraid something bad has happened. Would it not be well to find out about it?"

This the Warden promises to do, so I stifle my fears as best I can and turn to the events of the day. I report progress; and we again debate whether or not I had better make a change of

65

occupation. Last evening we decided that I should remain still another day in the basket-shop; for it seemed as if I were getting as much out of my experience there as I could anywhere. The Warden is inclined to agree with me that we have been singularly fortunate so far, in the working out of our plans, and that it might be a mistake to change. Jack Murphy, when I talked with him about it to-day, said, "What good would it do you, to go and work in a shop where you can't talk? You can learn everything there is to know about such a shop by spending ten minutes there, any time." Then he added, with a smile, "You know, Brown, we don't want to lose you here." I hope this last is true, and I think it is; but, aside from that, his reasoning impresses me as good.

So the Warden and I agree that I am to stay in the basket-shop at least another day, and he leaves me to my thoughts and my fears.

I shall now put away this journal, and prepare my bed for the night. I fear that my sleep will be haunted by echoes of those dreadful sounds.

It may be well to interrupt my journal here, and explain the noises of Wednesday evening. As will be seen in Thursday's journal, I heard many of the details the next day, but it was some time before I learned the whole story. I have examined personally several eye-witnesses of the occurrences and am convinced that the following statement is accurate.

There had lately been sent up from Sing Sing a young prisoner named Lavinsky. He is physically a weak youth; pale, thin, and undersized. His weight is about one hundred and twenty pounds; his age, twenty-one. On the charge of being impertinent to the officer of his shop, he was sent down to the jail, as the punishment cells are called, and kept there for five days in the dark on bread and water. Then he was allowed to go back to work. He did so, but was of course utterly unfit for work. The next day he was ill and remained in his cell, which was on the fourth tier on the south side of the north wing. This was on the opposite side of the cell-block from where I locked in, and a considerable distance down toward the western end of the wing; which accounts for my not hearing more distinctly the sounds which aroused in me such feelings of terror.

The day that Lavinsky returned to work was Tuesday, my second day in prison. On Wednesday he was afflicted with severe diarrhea all day, but for some reason, in spite of his repeated requests, the doctor was not summoned. The reason probably was that Lavinsky was in the state known in prison as bughouse—that is

66

to say, at least flighty if not temporarily out of his mind. He himself, as I have subsequently found in talking with him, has no very distinct recollection of the events of that Wednesday evening. If not out of his mind, he was certainly not fully possessed of it.

In the evening, after his failure to get the doctor, Lavinsky created some disturbance by calling out remarks which violated the quiet of the cell-block. I understand that the form this took was something of this sort: "If you want to kill me, why don't you do it at once, and not torture me to death?" He seemed to be possessed with the idea that his life was in danger. I do not know in what condition he was when first placed in jail, but I do know that the time he spent down in that hellhole, five days, was quite sufficient to account for his mental condition when he came out.

Now here was a young man, hardly more than a lad, in a sick and nervous condition that had produced temporary derangement of mind. What course did the System take in dealing with that suffering human being? Two keepers opened his cell, made a rush for him, and knocked him down. One eye-witness says that they black-jacked him, that is, rendered him unconscious by striking him on the head with the instrument of that name. During the brief scuffle in the cell the iron pail and the bucket were overturned. Then, after being handcuffed, the unresisting if not unconscious youth was flung out of his cell with such violence that, if it had not been for a convict trusty who stood by, he would have slipped under the rail of the gallery and fallen to the stone floor of the corridor four stories below, and been either killed or crippled for life.

Then the two keepers, being reinforced by a third, dragged their victim roughly downstairs, partly on his back, kicked and beat him on the way, and carried him before the Principal Keeper, who promptly sent him down to the jail again.

Let it be remembered that this poor fellow is a slight, undersized, feeble specimen of humanity, whom one able-bodied man ought to have had little trouble in handling—even if any use of force were necessary.

This scene of violence could not pass unnoticed; and the loud protests and outcries of the prisoners whose cells were near by, as they heard and saw the treatment accorded to their helpless comrade, were the sounds I heard far away in my cell. One of the trusties who, having the freedom of the corridors, was enabled to see most of the occurrence, so far forgot his position as to venture the opinion that it was a "pretty raw deal." This remark was overheard by an officer; and the trusty at once received the warning that he had better keep his mouth shut and not talk about what didn't concern him.

If it is realized that these officers have what almost amounts to the power of life and death over the convicts, it can be understood that such a warning was not one to be lightly disregarded.

Lavinsky, having been landed again in the jail, was kept there from Wednesday evening until Saturday afternoon. What special care or attention was given him during that time I am unable to state, but there is no reason to suppose that any exception was made in his case. Like the other denizens of the jail, he was fed only on bread and a very insufficient quantity of water—three gills in twenty-four hours—and also experienced the intolerable conditions of that vile place.

On Saturday afternoon, three days later, he was still down there, and still bughouse. Then as there was a disturbing rumor among the officials that I was planning to be sent to the jail, he was taken away about an hour before my arrival. His cell was the very one which I occupied, after it had been thoroughly cleaned.

He was removed from the jail to a special cell, where his case was taken up personally by the Warden, and where the poor youth was at last put under the care of the doctor, and received some humane and sensible treatment. When I first saw him, some three weeks after my term had ended, he had not become entirely rational, although he has since recovered himself. As I have already said, he had at first no clear recollection of the brutal treatment of which he had been the victim, nor in fact of anything that occurred at the time. Perhaps it was all the better that this was so.

An exceptionally intelligent convict, whose term expired soon after these events, and who could have had no earthly object in misrepresenting the matter, described to me after his release the episode in detail. He had been an eye-witness of the entire occurrence, as he was standing on the gallery where he could see everything that happened. He summed it up in these exact words: "Mr. Osborn, it was one of the most brutal things that I have ever seen, in all my experience in prison."

His story is fully corroborated by what I have learned, upon careful inquiry from other men.

Doubtless some will say that the statements of convicts are not to be believed. That touches upon one of the very worst features of the situation. No discrimination is ever made. It is not admitted that, while one convict may be a liar, another may be entirely truthful; that men differ in prison exactly as in the world outside. It is held, quite as a matter of course, that they are all liars, and an officer's word will be taken against that of a convict or any number of convicts. The result is that the officers feel themselves practically immune from any evil consequences to them from their own acts of injustice or violence. What follows from this is inevitable. Our prisons have often been the scenes of intolerable brutality, for which it has been useless for the victims to seek redress. They can only cower and endure in silence; or be driven into insanity by a hopeless revolt against the System.

Not so very long ago one of the prisoners at Auburn, on a hot night in summer, as an officer was shutting the windows in the corridor outside, called out from his cell, "Oh, Captain, can't you let us have a little more air?"

The officer promptly went to the tier of cells whence the voice came and made a chalk-mark around the keyhole of one of the locks. When a man is "round-chalked" he is not released when the rest of the prisoners are let out of their cells, but reserved for punishment. In this case the officer mistook the cell from which the voice had come, and round-chalked the prisoner who was locked in next to the one who had dared to ask for more air.

The next morning, finding that his neighbor was about to receive the punishment intended for himself, the culprit promptly told the officer that he was the guilty party, and if anyone was to be punished, he ought to be. This honorable action was allowed no weight. He had some of his hard-earned money taken away from him, three days of his commutation cancelled, and the disc removed from his sleeve as a mark of disgrace; in short, he was severely punished—as his innocent neighbor would have been, had he not prevented it by taking the punishment upon himself.

The point is this: that no convict has any rights—not even the right to be believed; not even the right to reasonably considerate treatment. He is exposed without safeguard of any sort to whatever outrage an inconsiderate or brutal keeper may choose to inflict upon him; and you cannot under the present system guard against such inconsiderate and brutal treatment.

I should not like to be understood as asserting that all keepers are brutal, or even a majority of them. I hope and believe that by far the greater number of the officers serving in our prisons are naturally honorable and kindly men, but so were the slave-owners before the Civil War. And just as it was perfectly fair to judge of the right and wrong of slavery not by any question of the fair treatment of the majority of slaves, but by the hideous possibilities which frequently became no less hideous facts, so we must recognize, in dealing with our Prison System, that many really well-meaning men

69

will operate a system in which the brutality of an officer goes unpunished, often in a brutal manner.

The reason of this is not far to seek—a reason which also obtained in the slave system. The most common and powerful impulse that drives an ordinary, well-meaning man to brutality is fear. Raise the cry of "Fire" in a crowded place, and many an excellent person will discard in the frantic moment every vestige of civilization. The elemental brute will emerge, and he will trample down women and children, will perform almost any crime in the calendar in his mad rush for safety. The truth of this has been demonstrated many times.

In prison, where each officer believes that his life is in constant danger, the keeper tends to become callous, the sense of that danger blunts his higher qualities. He comes to regard with mingled contempt and fear those dumb, gray creatures over whom he has such irresponsible power—creatures who can at any moment rise in revolt and give him the death blow. And as they undoubtedly possess that power, he is always fearful that they may use it, for are they not dangerous "criminals"? And undoubtedly there is basis for his fear, for some of those men are dangerous, rendered more so by the nerve-racking System.

I can conceive no more terribly disintegrating moral experience than that of being a keeper over convicts. However much I pity the prisoners, I think that spiritually their position is far preferable to that of their guards. These latter are placed in an impossible position; for they are not to blame for the System under which their finer qualities have so few chances of being exercised.

But I have been betrayed into rather more of a discussion than I intended, a discussion out of place in this chronicle of facts. I have inserted so much by way of explanation both of what I have narrated in the foregoing chapter and of what I shall have to tell in those that are to come.

Since the above was written I have run across a passage in a book on English prisons which confirms so strikingly one of the statements just expressed that room must be made for it. "The real atmosphere of Dartmoor," says the author, Mr. Albert Paterson, writing of Dartmoor Prison, "so far as the men responsible for its well-being and discipline are concerned, is that of a handful of whites on the American frontier among ten times their number of Apache Indians. 'We stand on a volcano,' an officer said to the writer in a matter-of-fact tone. 'If our convicts here had opportunity to combine and could trust one another, the place would be wrecked in an hour.'"

Aside from the author's ridiculously belated simile of the American frontier, we have here an accurate and forcible statement of the prison keeper's constant nervous apprehension of danger and the necessity of being prepared at any moment to sell his life as dearly as possible. And, of course, this feeling of the keeper increases his severity and the severity increases the danger, and so we have the vicious circle complete.

I am not now in any way disputing the necessity of a keeper being constantly on his guard, I am not saying whether this view of things is right or wrong, and when I use the word fear I do not mean cowardice—a very different thing, for a brave man can feel fear. I am simply trying to point out that in prison, as elsewhere, when men are dominated by fear, brutality is the inevitable result.

CHAPTER X
THURSDAY

In my cell, Thursday evening, October 2.

This morning is cloudy and dark; it has been raining heavily during the night, and the atmosphere is damp and oppressive. Oppressive too is the feeling left by the unexplained occurrences of last evening.

My first visitor is Officer X, the man who wouldn't answer my question last evening when he was standing back of the Warden and I asked him what that noise was. This morning he is exceedingly bland and also, like the weather, oppressive. He is so very anxious to know how I passed the night; and I tell him. He then says that a thousand people have inquired of him about me; and I remark that I'm glad my experiment is arousing so much interest. He then says that several men have said to him that I must have something special in mind, that I must be here for some ulterior purpose, and they believe the result will be some dismissals among the officers; to which I say that doubtless there are many people who, not having taken the trouble to read my address in the chapel last Sunday, although it was printed in the newspapers, are quite ready to believe anything except the simple truth.

He then enters upon a long rigmarole, the gist of which is how necessary it is for a man to do his duty; with which novel sentiment

71

I express my entire agreement. Then he adds that he has always been careful to do his own duty; upon which I make the startling comment that it is in the long run the best course to pursue. Then he casually turns the conversation around to show how closely connected he is to various admirers of my father and myself, and gracefully insinuates that he also shares these feelings; to which I can answer nothing, as this sort of thing always reduces me to embarrassed and wrathful silence. I hate to tell a man that he's a fool, and I hate quite as much to have him take me for one.

As the officer stands there talking, it is borne in upon me that he not only knows all about last night's disturbance, but that he was probably concerned in it, and is now deliberately trying to switch me off the track. He would not answer my question last night, and he avoids all reference to the matter this morning, substituting for the explanation which he knows I want, for he heard me speak to the Warden about it last evening, all this stuff I have outlined. Instead of being frank and telling the plain truth about last night's occurrence, he is trying to flatter me and pull the wool over my eyes.

He walks away and the taste in my mouth is not pleasant.

Soon Captain Kane unlocks the levers, and George presses them down to release us for a new day. I regret to say that I again create some confusion on the gallery by being late; but, as there is trouble with the lock on the tier around the corner, I catch up while the front of the line is held back by the delay.

Marching down the yard, my interest is aroused by a long, whispered conversation between Roger Landry at my side and Jack Bell who is immediately in front of him. Neither is farther than a foot or so away, yet my ears are not sensitive enough to catch a single word of what they say; and when I glance toward Landry I am unable to detect the faintest motion of his lips, although the talk is still going on.

Upon return from bucket duty I sweep out the cell, finding it for some reason especially dirty. Soon after I have finished this task, I come into possession, through a channel it is best not to specify, of an account of last night's performance, including the names of most of the actors. I judge that it is a bad business. This is the story as it comes to me. [9]

Three of the officers, among them X (just as I suspected), went into the cell of a young prisoner on one of the upper tiers of

_____

[9] This, of course, is the same incident that has already been given in the supplementary pages of the previous chapter, but I insert it again as a part of my journal. It illustrates the way news circulates about the prison.

the south side, hit him over the head, handcuffed and dragged him downstairs very roughly. His offense seems to have been that he is bughouse through confinement in the jail. So in their enlightened wisdom they have sent him back there; to cure him, I suppose, on the homeopathic principle, similia similibus curantur.

Before the march to breakfast George kindly brings me another package of sugar. It is evidently of distinct advantage, in more ways than one, to stand well with the trusties; I wish I knew them all, but possibly some may be afraid to show themselves at the door of my cell. I have a vague feeling that it is being closely watched.

Breakfast to-day consists of some kind of porridge, with the usual bootleg and punk. Thanks to George, I do not need the sugar which Landry again offers me; and, having more than enough for my own portion of porridge, I silently pass what I have left to my neighbor on the other side, who receives it without daring to express any evidence of gratitude.

Arrived back in my cell, George stops to have a pleasant chat with me, and tells me a little about himself and his experiences. Then, after the usual operations attendant upon our release from the cells, we march down the yard and arrive at the basket-shop, ready for the business of the day.

Murphy is on hand with his usual cheerful smile:

"Well, good morning, Tom."

"Good morning, Jack." And upon this more intimate footing we commence our fourth day's work together.

As I left a bottom incomplete last evening, I begin work with vigor in order to finish it; but unfortunately the rattan we are now using is so stiff and rotten that it not only breaks constantly and is very hard on the fingers, but makes good workmanship quite impossible. Finally we are compelled to stop altogether, while the withes are taken and soaked in hot water, instead of the cold water in which they have been lying over night. Once in a while we have been getting soft and pliable withes that make work easy and pleasant, but most of them have been very brittle and difficult to handle.

While we are waiting for material, I hear the name of Brown called out; and find that I am told off, along with Jack and a number of others, to help pull up another car. This time it is lumber and not coal; the identical lumber, in fact, that stood in front of the north windows and caused the P. K. such anxiety about our eyesight yesterday afternoon.

The gang is duly counted and handed over to the officer

73

charged with the job; and soon we are enjoying the exercise of successive tugs of war with the block and tackle, similar to those of Tuesday. It is not so hard a job as that was, however, there being but one car and that a comparatively light one; so Jack and I regret that our spell of exercise is not longer and stronger. It is far better than nothing, however, and we return, refreshed and invigorated, to our basket-work.

While we are waiting for working material, Jack approaches me cautiously, leaning against the table with a very listless air, as if nothing were further from his thoughts than a subject of serious import.

"Did you hear anything last night, Tom?" he asks, turning his face just enough in my direction to reach me with his voice, which is subdued to its lowest tone.

"Did I? I should think I did," is my low reply. "What can you tell me about it?"

Jack repeats the story substantially as I have already heard it. The affair happened in one of the upper tiers almost directly over him, but he could see nothing of it, and he only heard the details through others. He thinks it is a bad matter, and adds one new item of information. He says that a certain trusty has threatened to go to the Warden about the case; he told the P. K. to his face that he would do so, and the P. K. threatened the trusty with retaliation if he did; but that the man feels so outraged by the brutality he witnessed that he intends to do it in spite of the P. K. [10]

I know this particular trusty and should be sorry to have him get the ill-will of the P. K., or any of the prison authorities. So I decide to try to take steps to prevent this. Convicts, as I have already hinted, have underground means of communication of which the officials do not always know.

The truth of this last statement was demonstrated in an interesting way this morning. Strict orders were given by the Warden when I first came here that there was to be no photographing. We cannot prevent publicity about this affair of mine. But at least we can, and have, cut out the moving pictures; and discouraged other attempts to exploit and emphasize the personal side of it. It is not our fault if many of the newspapers print ridiculous statements which are not founded upon fact.

---

[10] There were some small inaccuracies in Jack's tale, especially this account of the trusty and the P. K. The facts are as stated in the last chapter. I have let this passage remain, however, as it represents what I heard and understood at the time.

74

I have, by the way, been seeing a number of newspapers, as the men in the shop are all keenly interested and are anxious to share with me any "Tom Brown dope" that comes their way. Every day half a dozen papers reach me in roundabout ways. I always read them, taking care to lurk behind a post or otherwise screen myself from the eye of the Screw. Captain Kane, like Captain Lamb, evidently feels that it is well to temper discipline with tact and discretion. He is firm in manner, quiet and self-contained, allowing no liberties from anyone, but evidently bent upon doing his duty and at the same time being kindly and fair in his treatment of the men.

What I started to say was that the order against photography was obeyed until to-day. There is doubtless a good reason for this morning's exception—I have to leave that for the Warden to explain; but while Jack and I were talking, one of the convicts passing behind me said in an undertone, "Look out, Brown! Camera inside."

In due course of time, Grant makes his appearance, showing around a visitor who carries a kodak. He makes no attempt to exercise the machine in our neighborhood, and is simply shown through like any other visitor. Not long after he is gone the hour of noon approaches. We form in due order, and, while awaiting the signal to start, for the first time I dare to turn my head sufficiently to get a good look at the dapper young prisoner who leads the right line of our company, the back of whose head and manner of marching had so pleased me. And whom should I discover him to be but my own boss, Harley Stuhlmiller. Here have I been three days marching behind him ten times a day, and seeing him at frequent intervals all day long in the shop; and now for the first time I am able to match his face and the back of his head together. This gives a good idea of the remoteness of man and man in this unnatural place.

We make our usual march down to the stands, where each man secures his bucket, and then back up the length of the yard.

Sure enough—there he is. The camera fiend is standing with Grant and some others just outside of the main door. Evidently he has not been told that at noon we turn aside to the door leading into the north wing; it is only at night that we march directly into the main building in order to secure our bread for supper. The men quickly catch the humor of the situation, and there is a deal of quiet enjoyment of the photographer's disappointment. He hastens down toward us, but only succeeds in snapping our rear ranks as we enter the building. Tom Brown has escaped him.

It is certainly wonderful how news gets about in this prison.

From what the Warden tells me this evening, it could not have been more than half an hour after the man with his kodak entered the front gate before the warning of his camera was received by me, over at the farther end of the yard. The Marconi system hasn't very much advantage in speed over the wireless telegraphy of the prison.

My first action upon getting back to the cell is to get my own telegraphic system in working order, so as to get word to that trusty who has threatened to go to the Warden about last night's occurrence. I want him told not to attempt to go over the head of the P. K., but to leave the whole matter to me. I send two messages through the secret channels and then get ready for dinner.

That meal, when we reach the mess-hall, turns out to be corned beef, potatoes, an excellent pickled beet, and the usual bread and coffee. I eat with more relish than usual, and find the time allotted for the meal altogether too short for a proper enjoyment of it. Or perhaps the word enjoyment is a little too strong—let us say, for a proper disposal of it.

Upon returning to my cell I find a piece of paper folded up to its smallest capacity lying on the floor. It is a note from one of my fellow prisoners—a kite, to use the proper term. I have been receiving such documents ever since I came. They reach me in all sorts of ways; all of which ways are of course forbidden. Some of the notes are business-like, some are rambling and incoherent, some are sad, some are humorous, all are characteristic and good tempered. The majority contain requests to see the writers, after I get through my bit. Some go into long accounts of themselves and their experiences. One has written a good-sized pamphlet, telling his life-story in considerable detail. All of them are filled with a pathetic sense of gratitude toward Tom Brown, their new pal. They seem to think that I am making an unheard-of sacrifice for their sakes.

It is curious how far away is the feeling of dread of this place that I used to have; that I must confess to have had even when I decided to come here. Exactly the same, I imagine, as one would feel about entering a den of wild beasts, except that these were capable of being talked to and reasoned with. I suppose I did have some little, a very little, notion of personal danger, which now seems wholly absurd. I have at present a sense of companionship and sympathy with these men, as warm and strong as I have ever felt anywhere. It is accompanied, of course, by a great feeling of pity for their mistakes, the bitterness of their expiation, and the well-nigh hopeless difficulty under present conditions of regaining their hold upon life.

76

After the regular period of rest in the cell after dinner, and my usual calls from the trusties, we march back to the shop. The routine is always the same. Again I hear the clicking far away to the left around the corner. Whereupon I rise from my shelf-table, unhook and drop it down, put away my writing materials in the locker, and don my coat and cap. Again the Captain passes by, unlocking the levers as he goes. He quickly finishes the remainder of the cells on this side of the tier, then repasses, pressing down each lever just long enough to allow the grated door to be pushed open by the prisoner waiting inside. Again I shove my door open as quickly as possible and follow immediately after the Captain; for all the men who belong in front of me in the line lock in farther along the gallery. When we reach their cells I drop behind enough to give them their proper places, and thus there is a minimum of disorder when we have descended the flight of iron stairs to the door and are lining up in double column for our march down the yard.

The marches too are always the same—day after day—with only slight variations; as for instance the one after breakfast when, as it is unnecessary to visit the sewage disposal building, we march directly to the shop. But this afternoon it is the same as all afternoons; short-step at first until all the company have reached the walk; then a rap of the keeper's stick and full-step down the yard; swing around to the left; through the sewage disposal building for the benefit of the few who bring down their buckets in the afternoon; a momentary pause at the stands and then away to the shop. As we go down the half dozen steps into the building we break ranks and Jack Murphy comes up from his place, somewhere in the rear, with his usual pleasant greeting.

"Well, Tom, how did you enjoy your dinner?"

"It was all right, only to-day I didn't have time enough to eat it."

"No, they cut us pretty short sometimes at dinner."

No incident of particular interest happens this afternoon. My fingers are getting rather stiff and sore, working with the hard and brittle rattan that they give us. It is discouraging to attempt good work with such material, but we do the best we can. Stuhlmiller has taken the matter up with John, the citizen instructor, whose last name I have not yet learned, and with Captain Kane. They are thinking about repairing an old vat where the withes can be properly heated and softened by steam. That is all right, but it won't help my fingers much, as I shall be out of here long before it is done.

About my going out there is a little joke. Every man wants to know how long I'm going to stay here. I tell them I don't see how I can remain beyond Sunday, as there is business I have to attend to in New York City next week. Whereupon Jack winks his eye and, speaking to the questioner in a loud whisper, says, "Oh, these new guys are always thinkin' they ain't going to stay long. New trial, or pardon or something. He'll be here for some time yet, so don't you worry. He's a little bug about going right out, you know." A joke which has its non-humorous side; founded, as it undoubtedly is, upon many a grim fact. As the Scotch saying runs, "A true joke is no joke."

In the course of the afternoon, talking again of last night's occurrences upon which no further light has come, I retail to Jack my visit from Officer X this morning, and that gentleman's conversation. At the conclusion Jack looks over to me with scorn on his honest face and blurts out, "Say! I wonder what they take you for anyway!"

"For a damn fool, evidently; that is, some of them do," is my answer. "But fortunately, Jack, they can't be all like that. Probably these officers last night were afraid that I should hear the disturbance that young fellow was making, and felt that they must hustle and get him out of the way on that account. At least that's how I am inclined to figure it out."

"Well," says Jack, "some of them seem awful anxious to know all about you. They come around to my cell every night and ask after my partner's health, and want me to tell them about everythin' you say and do. But you can bet I throw 'em off the track. Say," he continues, "I just wish you could have seen one of the screws last night when he asked me how long you were goin' to stay here, and I told him that from what I heard you say I judged it wouldn't be much over two months. Gee! but you should have seen his face! He was just horrified." And Jack laughs heartily at the recollection.

"Too bad to give the poor fellow a jolt like that. But after all, Jack, the keepers act a good deal as most any of us would in their places."

This kindly view is not perhaps altogether sincere on my part; but I do not wish to use my influence to stir up trouble between the keepers and the prisoners. Without standing up for the keepers when they are wrong—to do that would be to forfeit the confidence of my companions, I shall do my best to make the men feel that resistance to authority is both foolish and useless. Prisoners cannot expect to have things to their liking; but neither can keepers expect their charges to be blind to hypocrisy, or to acquiesce in brutality.

In the course of the afternoon I have a long and pleasant talk with Jack Bell. A convenient post is just at my right, behind which

Bell stands, screened from the view of the Captain. I can talk low without turning my head, and the officer cannot tell that I am not talking to Murphy. As everything else is going on as usual and the men working near pay no attention, not even looking at us, we are able to enjoy quite a prolonged conversation. Finally, however, the Captain seems to suspect something and steps down from his platform, but Bell glides off quietly and with an admirable innocent air of business. The Captain returns to his seat, apparently satisfied.

After Bell has dropped away, I have a long and interesting discussion with my partner. For some years I have felt that the principles of self-government, as developed at the Junior Republic, might probably be the key to the solution of the prison problem; but as yet I have not been able to see clearly just how to begin its application. There have seemed to be almost insuperable difficulties. In this connection Jack makes a suggestion which supplies a most important link in the chain.

In discussing the various aspects of prison life, the better and the worse, the harder and the less hard, we reach the subject of the long and dreary Sundays. Jack agrees with all those with whom I have talked that the long stretch in the cells, from the conclusion of the chapel service, between ten-thirty and eleven o'clock Sunday morning until seven o'clock Monday morning—over twenty hours, is a fearful strain both physical and mental upon the prisoners.

"Well, Jack," I say, "from what I have heard Superintendent Riley say, I feel sure he would like to give the men some sort of exercise or recreation on Sunday afternoons; but how could it be managed? You can't ask the officers to give up their day off, and you don't think the men could be trusted by themselves, do you?"

"Why not?" says Jack.

I look at him, inquiringly.

"Why, look here, Tom!" In his eagerness Jack comes around to my side of our working table. "I know this place through and through. I know these men; I've studied 'em for years. And I tell you that the big majority of these fellows in here will be square with you if you give 'em a chance. The trouble is, they don't treat us on the level. I could tell you all sorts of frame-ups they give us. Now if you trust a man, he'll try and do what's right; sure he will. That is, most men will. Of course, there are a few that won't. There are some dirty curs—degenerates—that will make trouble, but there ain't so very many of those.

"Look at that road work," he continues. "Haven't the men done fine? How many prisoners have you had out on the roads? About one hundred and thirty. And you ain't had a single runaway yet. And if there should be any runaways you can just bet we'd show 'em what we think about it." [11]

"Do you really think, Jack, that the Superintendent and the Warden could trust you fellows out in the yard on Sunday afternoons in summer?"

"Sure they could," responds Jack, his face beginning to flush with pleasure at the thought. "And there could be a band concert, and we'd have a fine time. And it would be a good sight better for us than being locked in our cells all day. You'd have fewer fights on Monday, I know that."

"Yes, it would certainly be an improvement on spending the afternoon in your cells," I remark. "Then in rainy weather you could march to the chapel and have some sort of lecture or debate; or Mr. Kurtz and I would come down occasionally and give you a violin and piano recital."

"Sure," says Jack; adding with a smile, "the boys would like that best of all, you know." (It takes an Irishman to slide in a delicate compliment in passing.)

"Well, that would all be first rate," is my interested comment; "but how about the discipline? Would you let everybody out into the yard? What about those bad actors who don't know how to behave? Won't they quarrel and fight and try to escape?"

"But don't you see, Tom, that they couldn't do that without putting the whole thing on the bum, and depriving the rest of us of our privileges? You needn't be afraid we couldn't handle those fellows all right. Or why not let out only those men who have a good conduct bar? That's it," he continues, enthusiastically warming up to his subject, "that's it, Tom, a Good Conduct League. And give the privilege of Sunday afternoons to the members of the league. I'll tell you, Tom! you know last year we got up an Anti-swearing League here in this shop, and we had a penalty for every oath or dirty word. The forfeits were paid with matches. You know matches are pretty scarce here, don't you? Well, we had a grand success with that

---

[11] There had been no runaways from the road camps at the time Jack was speaking. Before the camps were broken up at the end of the season, and the road work was suspended for the winter, there were four. Two were recovered and brought back; one returned of his own accord; and one made his getaway. The lives of the two who were brought back were made miserable by the abuse heaped upon them by their fellow prisoners for having violated the confidence placed in them. They finally petitioned the Warden to be transferred to some other prison.

league. But this Good Conduct League would be a much bigger thing. It would be just great. And go! sure it'll go."

"Well, Jack, perhaps you've hit the right nail on the head. We'll think it over, and talk more about it to-morrow."

Thus I close the conversation, wishing time to consider Jack's suggestion before we continue discussing a subject so big with possibilities. Sunday afternoon may be the key to the whole situation, and Jack may have found the key to the question of Sunday afternoon.

Toward the end of the day, when we have finished our work and Jack is sweeping up, I first read all the newspapers which have floated in my direction, and then take a long walk in stretches of ten feet or so. Our talk has given me much to think about. Jack, after finishing his sweeping, also walks, but in a different direction; for there is a strict rule that no two convicts may walk together. I manage at times to stretch my course a little, on one side or another, and whisper a word or two to some of the other prisoners. My remarks are always greeted with a ready smile and a pleasant gleam of the eye—even in the case of a poor fellow whose face shows that he is lacking in ordinary intelligence.

Closing time comes. "Good night, Jack!" "Good night, Tom!" (I got ahead of my partner this time.) We form in line; the old men and cripples start off first; the rest of us march up the steps and along the tracks; then after pausing at the bucket stands, swing up the yard to the main building; where I seize my bread, clamber up the iron steps; pass a whispered word or two to some of my special friends as we separate for the night; take my tin cup of fresh water which stands on the shelf; stand for a moment at the cell entrance watching the fellows pass who lock in around the corner; and then pull to my iron grated door, locking myself in for the night. I never perform this last operation and hear the click of the lever which announces that I am fastened securely in my cell, without a feeling of resentment. At least, if a man is to be caged like this, it ought to be done by visible exercise of authority. They shouldn't expect him to lock his own cage. Speaking as a convict, I call it adding insult to injury.

The following is Jack Murphy's description of the regular routine: "On reaching his gallery each inmate must go direct to his cell, closing his iron door to within an inch of the catch, where the lever falls in place. He must then stand with hands on his iron-grated door until the Captain (who is now on his way, locking up) reaches his cell; then the convict pulls in his door, the lever falls into

81

its catch and the Captain simultaneously inserts his large key into a lock at the side, locking the lever so that it cannot be raised. He then counts his company.

"The process of counting is done in this manner: the Captain, in passing each cell, takes hold of the lever while the inmate shakes his door vigorously. In this way the Captain does two mental things at one time, namely: he assures himself that each cell door is securely locked, and that his charge is behind that secured lock. This procedure is continued until the last cell and convict is counted. Then the iron bar which runs the length of the gallery is let down by a lever operated by the Captain at the end of the gallery. This bar runs in front of an iron rod or arm attached outward from the cell door. It is twenty inches long by half an inch square, and is fastened to the left side of the cell door.

"I forgot to say that, after the lever, which lowers the long iron bar, is pulled down, it is also treated to the lock-up system. A Yale lock is used for this purpose; so you see the poor dumb iron is even a victim to the Prison System.

"In case of illness, after the prison is closed for the night, an officer has to go to the trouble of running up to the front hall for the key of the gallery on which the convict is ill. This would take him 15 minutes to do; and after he got through unlocking all the locks and pulling the lever the convict might be fit for an undertaker instead of a doctor.

"A convict must not loiter on his gallery. This is considered by some captains a serious offense; and as for talking—good night! This last is as bad as if you were charged with talking out of your cell to your next-door neighbor. A report for such an offense would read something like this: 'Convict Brown is reported by Captain Jeff [or Mutt] for the following: Loitering on the gallery, talking and causing general disorder.' Next morning Convict Brown would hit the Booby Hatch for three or four days and a fine of $5.00."

Jack's statement is, of course, correct. I knew that I was taking a chance in whispering; but I got away with it, all right. So do others, including Jack himself.

To understand fully the Prison System it should be added that this long iron bar, which forms the third lock and about which so much fuss is made, only exists in the basement and second tier in the North Wing, and not at all in the South Wing. There is no discrimination made, by confining the more dangerous men in the extra-locked cells. But, gravely, every night and morning, that silly extra bar is lowered and raised for a small percentage of the prisoners—a ridiculous waste of time and energy.

This evening has been marked by a visit from the Chaplain, who has returned from Syracuse. He tells me that my experiment has aroused great interest among the clergymen assembled at a religious conference he has been attending; that he has had to answer countless questions. He also tells me that he is returning there again this evening and will telephone to the gentleman who was proposing to employ his assistant, Dickinson, and see if work cannot possibly be found for him. I tell the Chaplain of my letter, and beg him to add assurance of my own belief in the young man's stability and intention to do right.

Later the Warden comes. He brings me, as usual, a copy of the Auburn newspaper, so that I must set this down as the third exception that is made in my case. As a regular newcomer I should not be allowed a newspaper.

I ask the Warden about last night's disturbance. He has inquired into it, he says, and found it was only a case of a troublesome fellow, sent up from Sing Sing recently, who was making some little disturbance in the gallery. After they admonished him he wouldn't stop, so they had to take him down to the jail. When the officer entered his cell, he threw his bucket at the officer and there was a little row. "I'm inclined to think," adds the Warden, "that he may be a little bit crazy, and I'm going to look into it."

"I suppose that is the official version," I remark to the Warden. "Well, I certainly hope you will look further into it; for, speaking frankly, I think they are trying to slip one over on you. If my information is correct, and I believe it is, the case is rather different from what you have told me; and the treatment given the young fellow was inexcusably brutal."

I put the matter rather mildly to the Warden, for I don't want him to think that I am losing my balance and taking everything that is said to me by all my fellow-prisoners as gospel truth. To believe everything they say would doubtless be as stupid as to believe nothing.

The Warden and I again discuss the desirability of my working in one of the other shops during the remaining time here; but after full consideration we both feel that more is to be gained by staying where I am. There is only a day and a half left.

"You still feel, then, as if you wanted to try the jail?" asks the Warden.

"Yes, more so than ever," I answer, "for I must find out why the prisoners all speak of it with such horror. When you showed me the place last June, I thought it a very uncomfortable hole, and it was not pleasant to think about afterward. But there must be some such place to put men who defy all authority; and it didn't strike me as so very terrible. These fellows all speak of it with bated breath and a queer look in the eyes, as though it held some ghastly recollection. What can it be?"

"I'm sure I don't know," answers the Warden.

"Well, neither do I, and I want to find out. Of course," I add, "I'm not going to be foolish about the thing. If I find I don't feel well enough for any reason, when Saturday comes, I shall just cut it out. But if my physical condition continues as good as it is now, I mean to try it."

"All right," says the Warden. "I wanted to know, so that I can give orders to have one of those jail suits washed. There is no need of your running any unnecessary risk in the matter, and those dirty old clothes I don't like."

This is my first knowledge of the custom of giving the prisoners who are sent to the punishment cells clothes especially reserved for the jail; and my thoughts travel at once to the filthy and disreputable garments I had seen on a prisoner the Warden had once interviewed there in my presence.

"Well, I shall appreciate it if I can have a clean suit," I said. "There's no reason, I suppose, why I should not accept that exception."

So it is arranged. The Warden's visit comes to an end, and another day of my voluntary exile from society is closed.

Now for another long and restless night.

I shall not mind so much the periods of wakefulness to-night. Jack Murphy's Good Conduct League will give me plenty of food for thought. I believe he has struck the path for which I have been groping.

CHAPTER XI
FRIDAY

In my cell, Friday evening, October 3.

This morning breaks gray and cloudy again. I wake early and hear the night officer, some time before six o'clock, come and wake my neighbor in the next cell. He and I tap each other "Good night"

84

regularly now; and this morning I send through the stone wall a greeting for the day. He returns my message; and when the keeper comes again at six o'clock, this time to open his cell, he waits, apparently, until that officer's back is turned and then, putting his head only just so far past the opening of my cell that his voice can reach me, utters a hoarse and hasty "Good morning" and vanishes. This puts me in thorough good humor, and as I hear the factory bells and whistles greet the new morn I turn over to take just one final nap before beginning my own preparations for the day's work, wondering what new turn my adventure will take before night again falls.

Is it imagination, or is there more friendliness than usual in the nods and smiles which greet me from the faces upturned in the corridor below, as I traverse the gallery with my heavy bucket? It was extensively questioned among the convicts, in advance of my coming, whether I would do this particular part of the prison duty. As one of them told me, it was thought I would find some way to escape it; and the fact that I did not try to escape it, but assumed it cheerfully and as a matter of course, has much impressed them. As Joe put it to me three days ago, it was proof that I "meant business," and took the thing seriously, meaning to do exactly what I said—live the actual life of a convict up to the possible limit.

Bucket duty performed and while I wait in my cell for the breakfast hour, Dickinson comes running to my door. The good fellow has heard from the Chaplain that his job is ready for him and he can go out to-morrow. "And I can never be grateful enough to you, sir," he says with much feeling. "I shall never forget what you and the Chaplain have done for me; and I assure you you will never regret it, for I intend to go straight and show you that I mean every word I say."

"I'm sure you do; and I'm sure you will go straight," is my comment. "But how about your clothes? Have you anything but the prison suit you get on your discharge?"

"No, nothing."

"Well, but you can't go to work outside in those. People will spot you as an ex-con at once. Don't you want me to fix it so that you can get a decent suit?"

"Oh, if you only would!" is his heartfelt exclamation. "And, say, Mr. Osborne—pardon me—I mean Mr. Brown, if you'll please consider them not as a gift, if you'll let me have the money as a loan, I shall be greatly obliged. And I'll pay it back just as soon as I possibly can."

So we make arrangements by which he can be aided in this

way, and I sit down to write a note relative to the matter, but am interrupted by breakfast.

As we march to breakfast I try my hand, or rather my throat, at motionless conversation. Wishing to get word to one of the prisoners to procure a certain definite piece of information about the Wednesday evening incident, I seize upon a favorable moment to communicate with Roger Landry, who is marching ahead of me. In the faintest whisper and without moving my lips, I say: "Cun to ny cell a'ter dreak'ast." The ghost of a nod shows that he has heard and understood, and so we march in to our morning meal.

This time it is again hash, with the usual accompaniments— the rather sour bread and nasty coffee. (Whatever else changes, the bootleg remains the same.) The hash is better than that which we had for breakfast on—Wednesday, was it? I place aside only one piece of bone and one of gristle.

During the meal I look around more closely than I have previously done at the officers within my range of vision. There is one who wears a flannel shirt, and is so unshaven that he looks like a tramp. I'm glad I'm not under that Captain. At first I thought he was some one who had been drafted temporarily for duty, but I find he is one of the regular officers.

Here is an interesting psychological fact: that much as a man dislikes being treated as a slave, yet if he is to be so treated he wants his master to be the most efficient and best-looking master of the lot. I find myself comparing our Captain with this untidy-looking person in the flannel shirt, and having a distinct feeling of pride in the good looks and clean-cut appearance of our master. I know that if I were serving under that flannel-shirted and collarless officer I should have very little respect for myself and none for him. I don't know who he is, and he may be one of the kindest and best tempered of men; but I would be willing to wager that the prisoners under his charge are difficult to handle. It does not speak well for the general discipline of the prison that such a breach of official decorum should be permitted. The officer's cap on top of the unshaven face and the flannel shirt looks ridiculously out of place.

Soon after our return to the cells comes Landry, having understood perfectly my first attempt at convict conversation. I give him my message and he engages to see that it is delivered. As we are talking, another of the trusties passes by; and, before I can see who it is, a large sheet of paper is thrust under the door and the man is gone. I turn the paper over and on the other side is a most elaborate pencil sketch of myself, copied with extraordinary pains, apparently from some newspaper cut, and with it a slip of paper with this inscription: "Auburn Prison, September 30, 1913. To Hon. Thomas M. Osborne, Auburn, N. Y. As a memento of the days spent in our midst and sacrificed in our behalf. Auburn No. 31——."

Arrived at the basket-shop and soon after Jack and I have started working, I have a bad attack of nausea. I was very thirsty at breakfast time and inadvertently drank some bootleg. That must be the reason. No human stomach, without practice, can stand that stuff. I keep on working, hoping the feeling will wear off, but it does not. Then I walk up and down energetically while we are waiting for a new stock of rattan, but that has no better effect. Jack is much concerned and insists upon appealing to the Captain, who promptly sends to the hospital for medicine. In the meantime I go to the large door in the rear of the shop with a hope of relief from the cause of disturbance, but am only partially successful. A young prisoner who is washing windows asks me if I would not like some hot water. Indeed I would, it is the very thing I want. So he goes and gets it. He is a good-looking lad, a Greek, with the appealing eyes I have noticed in some of the Italian prisoners. I drink large quantities of hot water and rest awhile before continuing my work. Jack and all the other men about me are most kind and solicitous for my comfort, and I have never seen a more ready and friendly expression of sympathy. It is worth being ill to experience it.

The young Greek keeps my jar of hot water filled as fast as I empty it, and even before the medicine arrives from the hospital I already feel better. I take a dose, however, and go to work again. By the time the morning work hours are over I am in shape to march back to the north wing, although for a moment at the bucket stands I feel as if I were about to keel over.

In my cell I slump into the chair. (I don't think I have mentioned that the large chair which gave so much trouble on Tuesday night was replaced the next day by one of more manageable proportions.) I rest my head against the mattress, as it hangs over the bed, and feel ill for a few moments. But I take another dose of the Doctor's medicine and by the time the march to dinner comes I feel better; so much better that, carefully avoiding the bootleg, I manage to make a fairly good meal.

The menu to-day consists of very excellent hot soup, cold salmon, and pickles. I avoid the salmon and pickles, passing them along to another man, and contenting myself with the soup and sour bread. This passing to others of what one does not want seems to be very general. As it has to be done without visible conversation it is a little difficult for the newcomer always to know what is expected of him, and I'm afraid I have not always disposed of my meal to the

87

best advantage. I notice that Landry eats sparingly. As he has what might be called a semi-official position, I suspect that he reserves some of his gastronomic energies for the back pantry.

Again in my cell I address myself to sleep; and succeed in getting a brief nap, which is broken by my good friend Joe, who comes to make anxious inquiries after my health. He has heard that I am sick and is much concerned. I suppose he has learned it in the mysterious way so much news travels—by prison wireless.

I relieve Joe's anxiety; and then comes Landry with whom I have a pleasant talk on things in general, ending with religion. We are interrupted by the arrival of Captain Martin; and I am considerably amused at the deft way in which Landry has effaced himself and vanished before the officer regains his breath after climbing the stairs. Captain Martin comes from the Doctor to know whether I should like some milk.

"Thank you, sir, I think not now." I am on the point of adding that it would be extremely welcome this evening—well or ill; but the Captain does not offer it, and I do not quite like to ask for it. So I vouchsafe the information that I'm feeling better now and think I shall be all right in a very short while.

The Captain takes his departure; and my next caller is Dickinson, who is still radiant over the idea of leaving to-morrow. I give him the note I have written, which will enable him to get his clothes; and, when he tells me that owing to the late fine weather the authorities have refused to give him an overcoat, I add that item to his list.

When the time comes to go back to work I am feeling refreshed by my brief nap and the hour's rest after dinner. So I fall into line as usual with the company—I wonder what would happen if I stayed behind in my cell—and we march down the yard as usual. When I arrive at the shop, Jack is at my side in an instant.

"How are you feeling, Tom?" he inquires, anxiously.

I tell him that I am doing fairly well, and we set to work. In a very short time, however, the feeling of nausea returns; and Jack then gives me a remedy of his own which he says is often taken in the prison, where indigestion is only too common. It consists of bicarbonate of soda in vinegar and water. To show me that it is quite safe Jack takes a dose himself, I follow suit, and the result is satisfactory in both cases. I am also provided with plenty of hot water by my young Greek friend, who is apparently ready to take any amount of trouble for me.

While I am trying to do my fair share of the basket-making this afternoon one of my shopmates passes behind me and then pauses in the shadow of the post. "Say, Brown," he says, "you don't seem to realize that you are violating one of the fundamental laws of this institution, you're working too hard," and he goes off chuckling. I don't know that I am working too hard, but I do know that there seems to be about as little incentive to do a good, honest day's work as could well be devised. At a cent and a half a day the financial result is farcical, and my surprise is great that the state gets as good work as it does. Certainly it is far better than the state deserves. Looking about the shop I see a great many men who are doing their allotted tasks faithfully and well. Yet they have absolutely nothing to gain by it except the satisfaction of work well done.

In the course of the afternoon Jack and I resume our discussion about Sunday afternoons and the Good Conduct League. Further consideration has rendered both of us enthusiastic over the plan.

"Why, I know it would work, Tom," is Jack's decided statement. "The big majority of fellows in this prison the Warden don't have any trouble with. Well, just keep the rest of 'em out of the League. There's no reason why the men who are tryin' to make good should suffer because those miserable degenerates won't stand for what's right."

"Then you think that if the right men were trusted they could take care of the bad ones?" I ask.

"Sure!" replies my enthusiastic partner.

"Well, now let's see about this thing," I say, becoming more and more interested as the great possibilities of the plan present themselves to my mind. "Suppose it is Sunday afternoon and Superintendent Riley has given permission to use the yard. You can't have the officers coming back and spoiling their day off. How would you manage?"

"Why, just let the League fellows manage themselves," is Jack's answer.

"Yes, but how?" I persist. "You'd probably have an occasional fight of some sort, and you'd have to have some means of enforcing discipline. Could each company have a convict officer, a lieutenant to assist the regular captain?"

Jack looks grave. "That would be too much like Elmira," he says. "I'm afraid the fellows wouldn't fall for it. You know they just hate those Elmira officers; they're nothing but stool-pigeons."

Right here is where my Junior Republic experience comes to our aid.

"Yes," I say, "but we wouldn't have any Elmira stool-pigeons. Down there the inmate officers are appointed by the prison authorities, aren't they? Well, here we'd have the members of the League elect their own officers."

Jack stares at me a moment, and then his quick mind grasps the point. "That's it, that's it," he assents, eagerly, "we've got it now. Of course if the men elect their own officers they won't be stool-pigeons."

"Certainly not, they can't be," I rejoin, feeling now on familiar and secure ground, "for if the men elect them, they will be representatives of the men and bound to feel themselves responsible to the men. They may turn out to be poor officers— dictatorial, or weak, or incompetent—but they will not be stool-pigeons. Then you can guard against it still further by providing that whenever the men of a company lose faith in their officer he can be recalled and a new one elected."

As we discuss the matter new possibilities open up. Some sort of governing body of the League which shall plan ahead for its work, so that every Sunday something interesting may be presented. Perhaps the men might get up an entertainment themselves; or, as I suggest, possibly athletic sports on a holiday in the yard. This last makes Jack fairly gasp.

"Gee! I guess that we'd have everybody wantin' to join the League, all right," is his comment.

"And you really think the men would take an interest, and make such a thing go?" is my final question.

"Go!" says Jack. "The only trouble will be if we ever had a fight in the yard everybody'd want to stop it to show that they didn't stand for it. And I'm afraid that fourteen hundred men would come pretty near to putting the two fighters out of business."

"Well, then, let us think over this matter fully and carefully, Jack, and later on I'll take it up with you and see what we can work out of it. I think you've got hold of the right end and struck a big thing."

The next time Stuhlmiller comes to our table I say, "Harley, listen to this," and give him a rough outline of what Jack and I have been discussing. Stuhlmiller listens with smiling attention and gives the plan warm approval. This is encouraging.

On the other hand, when we open up the subject to Blackie Laflam, he takes a different view. He is quite ready to accept the blessings of Sunday afternoons in the yard or chapel; but he balks at the idea of inmate lieutenants.

"Cut it out," is his comment. "I wouldn't be bossed by no convict. Ain't the keeper enough? What's he paid for? No Elmira stool-pigeons for mine!"

So there we have the two views very well outlined, and the two currents of public opinion fairly contrasted. Harley sees the point at once, is ready to join in and accept the responsibilities which must go along with the privileges; Blackie has to overcome his prejudices and be convinced of the benefit which may accrue to him personally. We shall have to take into account both groups of which these two men are types. [12]

Except for these discussions this last afternoon passes without any new excitement. I find myself frequently wondering about to-morrow. In my present condition it would be very foolish to attempt the jail. Fortunately I am feeling better every moment, even if I am "working too hard"; perhaps because of doing so. By the time the order comes to fall in at the end of the afternoon I am quite myself again—thanks to Jack's remedy, the Doctor's medicine, and the Greek boy's hot water, to say nothing of the League discussion.

One incident of the afternoon touches me extremely. Working not far from us is a young lad from Brooklyn. He can't be more than eighteen or nineteen years of age—a good-looking youth, having no special friends apparently and speaking but little to any one. Every moment when he is not working he is either vigorously walking, or poring over some book, a lurid dime novel I should judge from its appearance. I have tried to make friends with him, but without much success. My advances are received pleasantly enough, but awaken apparently very little response. To be sure we do not have a chance to enjoy much real conversation, but his face does not light up as do those of most of the prisoners with whom I get the chance to exchange even a word or two.

This afternoon, while I am working away at the bench, I suddenly see a hand outstretched in front of me, and in its palm a small bunch of about two dozen green, dyspeptic-looking grapes. A more forlorn attempt at fruit I have never seen.

I turn, and it is my young friend of the dime novel. The lad has somehow or other come into possession of these sickly grapes, and is making to me the best offering he can. I dare say it sounds like a very commonplace occurrence, but in reality there is something infinitely pathetic in this poor imprisoned boy's attempt to express friendliness. I wish I could give him in return some of the real fruit that is at this moment wasting on the vines at home. As it is, I can only tell him that I do not dare eat fruit while my stomach is out of

---

[12] Both Stuhlmiller and Laflam were elected on the original committee which prepared the organization of the Mutual Welfare League, and have worked enthusiastically for its success.

order, but that I appreciate his kindness none the less. So he goes back to his exercise; and I am left wondering how in the world—or rather, how away from the world—did the boy come by those grapes. [13]

Thus I close my last full day's work in the shop. Where shall I be at this time to-morrow, I wonder? It occurs to me that this was the same question I was asking myself only five nights ago, before I came to prison.

We march back up the yard without incident; and in due time I regain my cell, after getting my bread for supper.

Here Dickinson comes again, to express his gratitude and have me share in his joy at deliverance. I say, "And now I suppose it's good-bye."

"Oh, no," he replies; "I shall come and see you again to-morrow morning before I go." Then he tells me all his plans, and how he expects to rejoin his wife and children. His joy is pathetic when one reflects upon the individual sorrows and disappointments that must await him, with always in the background the horrible dread of having his past discovered. Even his children do not know the truth; they think their father has only been away on a long journey. I give him my very best wishes and plenty of good advice, and again he assures me of his undying gratitude. It seems to be very easy to make these poor fellows grateful. Just a little human feeling, that is all that is necessary.

This evening, having little appetite and bread and water not seeming quite adequate to tempt what little there is, I turn to Landry's apples which have been awaiting just such an occasion. I eat one; and it goes to just the right spot. I have seldom tasted anything more delicious. On the whole, it appears well to be on good terms with a gallery man; and I can see that it would be especially so if he is the captain's trusty. I can imagine that then he might be of great service; or might, on the other hand, work one a deal of mischief if he wanted to. The trusty must have it in his power very often to prejudice the captain for or against certain prisoners by what he tells; and the captain would have no practicable means of verifying the trusty's statements. A system of petty and very exasperating tyranny would thus grow up. It is bad enough to be tyrannized over by an officer, but to be tyrannized over by an

---

[13] The mystery has been explained by one of my fellow-prisoners. "On the roof of the bucket-house and on the walls are some grape vines from which the sickly looking grapes are picked by the bucket-house man and given to friends. I tried them, but they were too much for me, and it's lucky you did not tackle them."

officer's stool-pigeon must be almost unendurable. While I have seen no examples myself, I imagine from what I have heard that this state of things is not unknown, as of course it is inevitable. One has only to recall one's own school days to know that.

After I have finished my supper of apples, bread and water, one of the trusties comes to the front of the cell, and I have a long talk with him. He grows confidential, and tells me his story. It is a mournful but perfectly natural one. An active boy, inclined to wildness; bad companions; a father whose business called him from home; a mother unable to cope with her wilful son; a life of dissipation; a picnic and drinking; a row with some other toughs; a handy pistol and an unpremeditated murder. Then comes the punishment which falls upon him, although others are equally to blame.

What surprises me about this, like other tales that have reached me, is the frank acknowledgment of the sin. There is usually an admission that punishment was deserved, occasionally an admission that on the whole prison has been useful—"I've learned my lesson"; but along with any such acknowledgment, an expression of intense resentment at unintelligent treatment and unnecessary brutality.

The tales of this brutality are almost beyond belief. They do not come out directly, put forward to arouse sympathy; very far from that. They crop out incidentally in the course of conversation and are only related when I ply the prisoner with questions. One man tells of being sent to a dark cell because he would not reveal to the warden something he did not know, and therefore could not reveal, about one of his fellow prisoners.

"Didn't you really know, or wouldn't you be a stool-pigeon?" is my natural question.

"I really didn't know," replies the trusty.

But the warden chose to think that the poor fellow did know, and sent him to the dark cell on bread and water for eight days. Then he was brought up, more dead than alive, given a single meal, and sent back to the dark cell for twelve days more.

Twenty days in darkness—on bread and water—for withholding information which he did not possess.

(It should be added that this did not happen under any warden now holding office.)

What are men made of who can treat human beings like that? I supposed that the Middle Ages were safely passed; but here is the medieval idea of the torture chamber to extract information right over again.

Then there is that other story of the man who committed suicide in the jail. This is what is told to me:

A number of years ago a poor fellow was sent here. His first night in prison was so terrible a nervous strain upon him, as it apparently is to all prisoners, that he could not keep from hysterical crying. The officer on guard ordered him to stop, but he could not control himself. So the officer chalked him in.

The next day he was reported for punishment and sent down to the jail, although he protested that it would kill him. That night he strangled himself with his handkerchief.

It is the jail which, apparently, either sends a man bughouse, or which lays such a foundation that he becomes so later on. But even when the time spent in the dark cell is short, as in Jack Murphy's case, who spent only eight hours there, there seems to be left an impression of horror—for which I find it difficult to account. I certainly cannot make a full test of prison life without having a jail experience. For me surely it can hold no such horror as for these poor fellows who are kept so many days on starvation diet. Yes, if I do not feel physically unfit to-morrow I must undertake the experience.

Soon after eight o'clock the Warden and Grant appear at my cell door. My ears are becoming sharper, I think. I can tell now the moment the door opens into the corridor below whether or not it is the Warden that is coming. Of course he arrives about the same time every evening, but also about this time the door is opening and closing a number of times. I recognize also the Warden's footfalls on the stone pavement below. It would not be very long, I imagine, before I should have a hearing as acute as my fellow prisoners seem to have.

The Warden begins with an apology. "I'm very sorry," he says, "but I forgot your newspaper to-night." Then he adds the usual remark, "I don't know how I came to forget it."

"Don't worry," I say, "it doesn't make any difference. I've read it."

The Warden stares at me incredulously. "You've read it! To-night's paper?"

"Certainly," I answer, "from beginning to end. Don't you believe it?" And in proof of my statement I produce the paper.

The Warden gasps. "Well, how in the devil did you get that?"

"Oh, come now! Don't you understand that I'm a convict?" I say jeeringly. "You mustn't expect me to answer such a question."

The Warden takes it all in good part. "Well, Dan," he says, turning to Grant, "this man seems to be on to the game all right.

What shall we do to him for violating the rules and smashing our system?"

"Don't you know," I remark with a serious air, "that so long as you hold me a prisoner I don't care a pin for your rules, and even less for your damn'd system. What do you say to that?"

"I say you're a dangerous man, and the sooner we get you off on parole the better," laughs the Warden. "But you will have to promise you won't make more trouble for us after you get outside."

"Oh, you're in for trouble, all right; whether I'm inside or out." I say it in jest, but we know there is many a true word spoken in that way. The Warden will have many new problems to handle while he is in office; for the old way is worn out and the new way is surely coming. Fortunately he is a genuine progressive and the new has no terrors for him.

Taking up the serious part of our business, the Warden says he must go out of town again to-morrow; and be gone over Sunday.

"What about that poor fellow they dragged down to the jail night before last?" I ask.

"Oh, you're all wrong about that matter," the Warden answers. "He was insolent and violent, flung his bucket at the keeper's head, and there was nothing to do but punish him. I've inquired into it and the officers were all right."

"You are being deceived," is my comment. "These men realize they are in bad. They're afraid of the truth; and they're steering you wrong. Take my word for it, Warden, there is more in that affair than they are permitting you to know. And you are up against the System as well as the prisoners themselves."

The Warden is troubled, no man has a heartier dislike of being made the victim of dishonesty or hypocrisy than he. "Well, what had better be done?" he asks. "I shall be very busy to-morrow before I go."

"Suppose we wait then," I suggest. "The man is probably not being abused now, wherever he is; and after I get out of here you can have a thorough examination made. I can guarantee plenty of material to enable you to get to the bottom of it."

"I am more than ever sorry I have to go away," says the Warden. "Now how about the jail? Are you still determined to go there? And, if so, how do you propose to be sent?"

"Well, as you know, I don't wish to be a fool about this thing, nor do I want to run any unnecessary risk. To-day I felt very sick; and, to be quite frank, if I should feel to-morrow as I did to-day I couldn't be hired to go to jail. But I feel so much better to-night that I think I shall be in good condition to-morrow. So what I propose is this. Let Dan come here to-morrow noon, and if I feel all right we can put through our plan. I did intend to go down to the jail to-morrow morning, so as to have the whole twenty-four hours there; but it would be better to wait until after dinner. There is no use in taking too large a dose. I ought to get all necessary information in— say, four hours.

"Some time in the afternoon, then, I will simply strike work. Grant can tip off the Captain; and he will send me to the P. K. Of course, if a fellow refuses to work, the only thing they can do is to send him to the punishment cells. If you were to be here I had thought of putting in a warden's call; and then of being so insolent to you that you would have no recourse but to order me punished. I should quite enjoy telling you what I think of your rotten old institution. But if you're going away that plan's no good, so we'll try the other."

"I think your present plan is better," says the Warden. "I should hate to have you tell me what you really think of us. Well, that ought to work out all right. Now how long do you say you want to stay there?"

"Well, I don't know that I'm anxious to stay any longer than just to get a good idea of what the place is like. I want to feel the flavor of it. But if I should be down there alone, it won't be very exciting. Suppose I go down about four o'clock; and Dan can come down and let me out about eight, or half-past seven, or say, seven. I think three hours will be a big enough dose."

"I've ordered some clothes cleaned for you," says the Warden, "so those are all right. Well, Dan," he adds, turning to Grant, "is everything perfectly clear?"

Thus it is arranged. I say good-bye to the Warden; and tell him that the Chaplain has asked me to say a few words to the men in chapel on Sunday. The Warden thinks it a good idea, and adds that the details about my leaving the prison can be arranged with Grant to-morrow. The general plan is that I shall go out on Sunday, marching back with the men after the chapel exercises. I can then take my belongings from the cell and go quietly up to the Warden's quarters, where I can wash and dress.

Our plans being thus settled, my visitors depart. Now to bed to see if I can get a good sleep in preparation for the most exciting part of my exciting adventure.

It is curious how far I have fallen into the prison rut. In the evening I find myself no longer thinking of my home or wondering what my family and friends are doing, unless I make a conscious mental effort. The tendency of this life is always to flatten one's thoughts, like one's actions, to a gray uniformity—a deadening routine.

Another sign that I had better be getting away from this place: I am losing all respect for authority of every kind. It is a mistake to suppose that rigid discipline increases respect for authority; it usually does nothing of the sort. In this place it increases disrespect, for many reasons which it is unnecessary to mention here. Whatever the reasons, the fact is undeniable. I believe every man in this place hates and detests the system under which he lives. He hates it even when he gets along without friction. He hates it because he knows it is bad; for it tends to crush slowly but irresistibly the good in himself.

CHAPTER XII
SATURDAY

In my cell, Saturday noon, October 4.

This morning,—the morning of my last full day in prison,— dawns bright and sunny; a pleasant change from the dark, cloudy and oppressive weather we have been having. The routine of my day has become firmly established now; and I conform to it almost without thought. At six I arise. As I sleep in my one suit of underclothes, my dressing may be said to have already begun. I add my socks and the clumsy state shoes, which are on the chair close at hand. Then I am ready to stand upon the stone pavement of the cell. After this I gain space, and at the same time put my house in order, by hanging up mattress, pillow and blankets, and turning the iron bed up under them against the wall. Then I brush my teeth, wash my face and comb my hair. Then I finish dressing by putting on shirt, trousers, coat and cap. These and other necessary operations completed, I am ready for the day.

In the midst of my toilet the electric light is switched on; so that the latter part has been accomplished with its aid. As I have dressed leisurely there is not very long to wait before I hear the clicking, which marks the unlocking of the levers, far around the corner to my left. Already, however, I have heard the tread of shuffling feet in the corridor below; and know that the first company has already started down the yard.

All the familiar sounds,—the familiar routine,—seem to give me a sort of strange, new feeling on this last day. It seems so curious that something which now seems like the established order of the universe should ever have been unfamiliar, or that it should so soon come to an end—at least, so far as I am concerned.

The levers click; the captain unlocks the cells; the long bar is raised; the doors are opened; the galleries are filled with hurrying figures carrying the heavy iron buckets; and my company forms at the foot of the stairs.

What special reason there is for so much haste I have not yet discovered; but I presume that the officers put off their arrival at the prison to the very last moment, allowing the shortest possible time for the operations between their arrival and breakfast.

The air and sunshine are pleasant and invigorating as we march down the yard and back, emptying and leaving the buckets as usual. Then to my cell where I sweep out and shut myself in.

Soon comes breakfast with its regular routine. I have laid off my cap; as the lever is pressed down I push open the grated door, let Stuhlmiller, Bell and the other two who march in front of me pass by; then fall in between them and the next man. We traverse the short gallery to the right, descend the iron steps and line up in the corridor; standing motionless, with folded arms. As the Captain's stick strikes the stone pavement the line begins to move. Then at a second rap we march rapidly to the mess-hall. Just within the door we salute the P. K.; then swing to the right, turn to the left, pass alongside the men who have already taken their seats and are eating, and reach our shelf or table. As we stand at our places, comes one rap; and we lean down and pull out our stools, standing again erect. A second rap; and we sit. Throughout the meal the Captain stands, rigid and silent, in the aisle at our right.

Our Saturday breakfast is rice; which I eat with relish. My appetite is in excellent working order this morning, after a good night's rest; and I am feeling in fine physical condition. There can be no question about the punishment cell; no one who feels as well as I do has any excuse for not misbehaving himself. In dressing this morning I took up my belt another notch. My youngest was quite right when he asserted that I should not be so fat when I came out; I must have lost several pounds.

I carefully avoid the coffee this morning; no more bootleg for me! I reserve my thirst for a good drink of water when I get back to the cell.

Already, while we are stowing away our breakfast, the companies in our rear are departing; and now our turn comes. One rap; and we rise and set back our stools. A second rap; and spoons in hand (no use for knives and forks at this breakfast) we march in double file down the middle aisle,—holding our spoons high for the officers to see and dropping them into the proper receptacles at the door. Then back through the stone corridor, up the iron stairs and along the gallery to the cells. In these, as there is the wait of half an hour or more before shop-time, we are double-locked.

And now comes Dickinson, to wish me a final good-bye. He is in his citizen's clothes, and can hardly wait to have the gate shut behind him.

He assures me again of his desire and intention to go straight and make good; and I put through the bars two fingers which he grasps as fervently as he would my whole hand, if he could get it. Another moment, and the brave, well-meaning fellow is gone. If a man like this does not succeed, it is not his fault; but the fault of the System which fails to strengthen his power of self-control and ability to bear responsibility.

After Dickinson's departure comes one of the trusties, bringing the information which I passed the word along yesterday to get for me. Then I write in my journal and read some of the kites which have reached me. The latest one I find under the blankets,—tucked into the strap which holds up my mattress—a most ingenious hiding place.

Then comes work-time. Again the captain unlocks the levers; and again I follow along the gallery to the iron stairway and the yard door. After a much shorter period of waiting than at our earlier march, we start off and go directly down the yard and around the corner to the basket-shop.

"Good morning, Tom!" "Good morning, Jack!" and we are off to work in good time.

"Well, old pal, how are you feeling to-day?"

I look up and catch an anxious look in my partner's eyes. I laugh as I answer: "Oh, I'm all right; and in fine fighting trim."

I know what he means; and he knows what I mean. It is the shadow of the jail that is between us.

"Come on now, Jack," I say; "don't worry about me. I shall get through it all right."

"But you don't know what it means," he insists anxiously. "One hour of that misery is worse than a week of the worst kind of pain. You'd better think it over."

"Well, I'll tell you, Jack; I have reconsidered it and I don't believe I shall stay so long as I intended. In fact I had planned to go down this morning but I shall wait until afternoon. I'll get all I want of it in about three or four hours."

"You can just bet you will," and Jack turns away with a discouraged air to pick up a fresh batch of rattan. I'm afraid he thinks me a very obstinate and unreasonable person.

The rattan seems to be worse than ever this morning. They've tried cold water, and they've tried hot water, and they've tried steam; but like the White Queen's shawl, "there's no pleasing it." It still remains quite unfit to work with; and for the sake of the future usefulness of my fingers I can't help thinking it's just as well that my prison bit is drawing to a close.

As we are working away, one of our shopmates comes over to me (the same who accused me yesterday of working too hard) and says: "Well, Brown, I think you must be taking in the jail to-day."

My surprise is great. No one, except Jack, Grant and the Warden, were aware of my intention, so far as I knew.

"What made you think of that?" I ask.

"Oh, they had a jail suit washed yesterday; so I guess they're getting ready for you," is the reply.

These men are certainly sharp. They can "see a church by daylight."

We work busily at our basket-making through the morning, Jack and I—our last day together. I am actually beginning to feel that, if it were not for the pressure of business in my office and some engagements in New York City next week, I should like to stay longer among these new friends. But it may not be. I have secured what I came for—far more than I expected. And now the next question is: what can be done with this knowledge? How can it be utilized for the state? and incidentally to help these men who need help so badly?

The noon-hour approaches. "Is it good-bye, now, Tom?" says my partner, sadly.

"Oh, no," I answer. "You don't get rid of me so easily as that. I shall be back this afternoon."

Jack looks relieved; and we fall into line as usual—the last time I shall march out of the shop with these men, my close prison companions of six days.

Down to the bucket stands; up the yard; into the north wing; up the iron stairs; along the gallery; and around the corner to my cell. Then off with my cap and coat; some water on my face; a comb passed through my hair and I am ready for dinner. I have time to write a few paragraphs in my journal before we march to the mess-room.

100

For dinner roast beef, potatoes and some sort of preserve; quite the best meal we have had. I must eat enough to last over until to-morrow morning; although for that matter the supper in jail will be similar to those I've had every day—bread and water. But I feel as if the ordeal I am to pass through may need all my strength. So I make good use of my knife and fork; and again find the dinner time almost too short for a square meal.

Back to the cell, where I arrange everything for an indefinite absence. Then, as I am writing in my journal, I am interrupted by the arrival of Grant. He comes to find out if there is any change of mind on my part regarding the jail; and, if not, to make final arrangements. I tell him I never felt in better health; and that I'm ready to carry out the plan made last night. "I will strike work," I tell him, "between half past three and four; and be sent to the jail. You had better come for me there about seven o'clock. Don't make it any later," I add, "because I certainly will have had a sufficient taste of it by that time; and I see no reason for remaining any longer than is necessary. So please be on time."

Somehow Jack's warnings and admonitions, while they have not turned me from my purpose, have produced a feeling of disinclination to stay in the jail beyond a reasonable time. What is to be feared I am sure I do not know; or even that I fear anything. It is certainly not the pleasantest place in the world; but—well! I simply cannot understand why these men all speak of it in the way they do.

So Grant goes away; and now I close my journal. To-morrow morning I shall be too busy to write in it, as I shall be preparing the remarks I want to make to the men in chapel; that is, if the chaplain holds to his suggestion of calling upon me. I never like to attempt a speech of any kind unprepared; even an extempore and unexpected speech is so much better for a little preliminary improvising.

So here I write the last page within the walls; and go forth from my cell to embark upon the last round of my great adventure. I never expected to end my prison term with regrets; and I am probably the first man who ever did.

At the end of the gallery I hear the familiar sound of the key turning in the locks; so here go for the last time my pencils and paper into the locker, as I put on my cap and coat and prepare to follow the Captain to my final hours in the basket-shop.

Thus far my prison journal carries us. From this time on, for reasons which will be apparent, I have to depend upon subsequent memory. It is only fair to say, however, that it is memory made peculiarly clear by the unusual character of the circumstances.

The Captain unlocks the levers; the cells are opened; and we march down to the shop. With a serious face and without his usual greeting Jack joins me at our work-table.

In fact Jack is not in very good spirits; and I have to do most of the cheerful part. This is not surprising; when one thinks it over. A rather exciting episode in Jack's life is coming to an end; while the most exciting part of my adventure is just beginning. After that, I am going out, my life enriched with an unusual and interesting experience; while he is going back to the old, dull, depressing routine. Is it any wonder that he feels gloomy?

For about two hours, from half past one to a quarter past three, we both work away faithfully on our basket-making; and then as I finish off my last bottom I turn to my partner. "Well, old man, the time will be here pretty soon; and I may as well get ready for it. I think I'll go over and wash up."

So I raise my hand for permission; and upon seeing the Captain nod, as I suppose, I take Jack's soap and towel which we still use in common and go to the sink. On my way back, as I pass the Captain's desk, he stops me. "Brown, don't you know that you mustn't leave your place without permission?"

"Yes, sir," is my reply, "but I raised my hand."

"I didn't see it."

"Why, I thought I saw you nod, sir."

"I did not."

"Well, I am sorry, sir." Then it occurs to me that this reprimand gives a good chance to settle the jail matter at once. Feeling somewhat surprised at my own boldness, I assume a rather insolent air and remark, "But it makes very little difference; because I've decided that I'll not work any more."

"What do you mean?"

"I mean that the rattan has been very stiff and rotten, and my fingers are getting badly swollen and blistered. We have complained but it doesn't seem to make any difference. The rattan is as bad as ever; and I shall not go on with it."

"Do I understand that you refuse to work?"

"Well, that's about the size of it."

There is an instant's pause. Then——

"Go and get your coat and cap."

The foregoing colloquy has been carried on in low tones for I have no wish to disturb the shop, or make a show of rebellion. [14]

I make my way back to our work-table. "Well, Jack, I'm in for it!"

"What did you tell him?"

"I refused to work any longer."

"Gee! You'll get it in the neck, sure enough. You've committed a serious offense."

"That's all right; but I wish my hands weren't so sticky. I can't get them clean with that cold water."

"I'll get you some hot water."

Jack goes off to fulfill his errand; and I see that Grant has come into the shop and is talking to Captain Kane. Wondering if this is the first the latter has heard of my plan of action, I take my coat and cap down from the hook and put them on. The men begin to feel that something is up; and a number of them cease work and stare as an officer steps up to our table.

"Thomas Brown."

"Yes, sir."

"Come with me."

For a moment I wonder what he would do if I refused. I should like to try; but reluctantly conclude it would be better not. I turn and get one last glimpse of Jack's mournful face, as he stands at a distance with the pail of hot water which he has just secured. Waving my hand to him and stepping off in front of the officer, I make my way out of the shop in the face of its surprised inmates.

In this order we traverse the yard; and again, as on the day of my advent, I feel strangely conscious of many sharp eyes looking out from the various buildings. It is about half past three o'clock.

Just at the end of the south wing is a low building faced with stone, upon the ground floor of which is the jail office. The keeper who has me in charge guides me in and orders me to sit down. I do so. He then exchanges a few words with Captain Martin, who presides at the desk; hands him a yellow slip of paper and disappears up the yard toward the main building.

As I have said before, the one necessary virtue of prison life

---

[14] As a matter of fact I was testing the Captain's mettle far more than I supposed, for Grant's warning to be on the watch for such a move on my part had not yet reached him, as I thought it had. All the more must one admire the admirable way in which Captain Kane handled the matter. He showed himself cool and collected under rather embarrassing circumstances, for which he was totally unprepared. An excellent officer.

seems to be patience. I sit, and sit; and my sitting continues, as Mark Twain says about the circular staircase at Niagara Falls, "long after it has ceased to be a novelty and terminates long before it begins to be a pleasure."

In the meantime, the members of the coal gang, returning from work to their cells in the south wing, pass by the door and, looking in, see me awaiting my doom. There is deep surprise on the faces of most of them. The young negro who offered me his mittens, the day we moved the coal cars—Tuesday morning, I think it was, but it seems a long time ago—gives me a cheering nod as he begins to climb the stairs. Then Captain Martin, noticing the attention I am attracting, shuts the door. But it is too late. Undoubtedly the wireless has flashed the message, "Tom Brown's pinched," into every nook and corner of the prison by this time.

At last the P. K. makes his appearance. He takes his seat with an assumption of great dignity in an arm chair; and I rise and stand silently before him. He examines at leisure the yellow slip of paper which Captain Martin has handed to him, and clears his throat. "Thomas Brown," he begins, "you are reported for refusing to work"; and he looks up interrogatively.

"Yes, sir."

"What have you to say for yourself?"

"Well, sir, the rattan has been so stiff and rotten that we couldn't do good work, sir; and you can see for yourself that my fingers are getting swollen and blistered."

"You should have made a complaint to the Captain."

"So we did, sir; but it didn't make any difference. So I just told him that I wouldn't work any more."

There is a moment's pause.

"Well, Brown, this is a very serious offense—refusing to work; and, if you persist in it, I fear you will have to be punished."

"I can't help that, sir."

"Do you still refuse to work?"

"Yes, sir. I shall not work under existing conditions in the shop."

"Well, Brown; I'm very sorry to punish you; but I have to obey the orders laid down in such cases by those in higher authority than I am. Captain Martin, you will take charge of this man."

The P. K. takes his departure. Captain Martin leisurely unhooks a large key from a locker behind his chair and saying briefly: "In here, Brown," opens a solid iron door in the wall. We are in the passage which leads to the death chamber; that terrible spot where those who are adjudged guilty by Society of coldly calculated

104

and brutal murder are by coldly calculated and brutal murder put to death by Society. As if one crime of such nature done by a single man, acting individually, can be expiated by a similar crime done by all men, acting collectively!

We traverse the passage, up to the very door of the death chamber. Here is another iron door on the right. This is unlocked and opened; and we enter the jail.

It may be well, before beginning the next chapter, to explain just what the jail is like.

Up to the advent of Superintendent Riley, there were in Auburn Prison two types of punishment cells: the jail, and the screen cells. The latter are built into the regular cell blocks and are about three and a half feet wide with the same length and height as the regular cells. They have solid doors of sheet iron pierced by a few round holes about the size of a slate pencil. These holes are probably of comparatively recent origin. The doors of similar cells at Sing Sing and Dannemora had no openings except for a small slit at the extreme bottom and top.

Ventilation there was none; the occupant breathed as best he could, lay on the damp stone floor and went insane for lack of light and air, within full hearing of the officers—and incidentally of the other prisoners. The use of the screen cells at Auburn was ordered discontinued by Superintendent Riley immediately after he had seen and condemned those at Dannemora.

The jail at Auburn is at present the place where all offenders against prison discipline are sent for punishment.

Whether the offense is whispering in the shop or a murderous assault upon an inmate or a keeper, the punishment is exactly the same—varying only in length. So far as I can learn, there is no specific term for any offense; so that when a man goes to the jail, he never knows how long he may be kept there. The official view, as I understand it, is that no matter what the cause for which the man is sent to the jail, he had better stay there until "his spirit is broken."

The jail is admirably situated for the purpose of performing the operation of breaking a man's spirit; for it has on one side the death chamber, and on the other the prison dynamo with its ceaseless grinding, night and day. It is a vaulted stone dungeon about fifty feet long and twenty wide. It is absolutely bare except for one wooden bench along the north end, a locker where the jail clothes are kept, and eight cells arranged in a row along the east wall and backing on the wall of the death chamber. The eight cells are of solid sheet iron; floor, sides, back and roof. They are studded with rivets, projecting about a quarter of an inch. At the time that Warden Rattigan came into office there was no other floor; the inmates slept on the bare iron—and the rivets! The cells are about four and a half feet wide, eight feet deep and nine feet high. There is a feeble attempt at ventilation—a small hole in the roof of the cell; which hole communicates with an iron pipe. Where the pipe goes is of no consequence for it does not ventilate. Practically there is no air in the cell except what percolates in through the extra heavily grated door.

In the vaulted room outside there are two windows, one at either end, north and south. But so little light comes through these windows that except at midday on a bright, sunny day, if you wish to see the inside of the cells after the doors are opened you must use the electric light. There are two of these and each is fastened to a long cord, so that it can be carried to the farthest of the eight cells. At the south end of the room is a toilet seat, and a sink with running water where the supply for the prisoners is drawn. Up to the time of Superintendent Riley's and Warden Rattigan's coming into office, the supply of water for each prisoner was limited to ONE GILL FOR TWENTY-FOUR HOURS!

The sink was not used for the prisoners to wash, for the simple reason that the prisoners in the jail were not allowed to wash.

Other peculiarities of the jail system will be made clear in the next chapter.

CHAPTER XIII
A NIGHT IN HELL

As Captain Martin and I traverse the long stone passage leading from his office to the death chamber, I listen intently to catch any sound from the jail, for I am wondering whether or not I shall have any companions in misery; but nothing can be heard. Even when the Captain unlocks and opens the door on the right at the end of the passage and I step into the dungeon, there is no indication of any other inhabitants. Except for our own movements the silence is complete, although there is a peculiar reverberation of the vaulted roof which reëchoes every sound we make. I am aware of a sort of uncanny feeling about the place, as though there were some sort of living creature—man, ape, or devil—in every cell, with his face close to the bars, peering through and holding his breath.

The Captain, going to a locker which is at his left, backing against the iron wall of the first cell, opens it and takes out a shirt, trousers, coat, cap, and a pair of felt shoes.

"Take off your clothes and put these on," he says briefly.

I take the clothes as he hands them to me and place them upon a bench at my right, where I also sit and proceed to make the required change. If these are the clothes which have been carefully washed and cleaned for me, I should like to examine—at a safe distance—the ordinary ones. They must be filthy beyond words. And I suppose no one but a prisoner ever wonders or cares about the condition of the last man who wore them.

I take off my gray uniform, shirt and shoes, and as I stand in my underclothes the Captain feels me all over from head to toes to find out whether I have concealed about me a weapon or instrument of any kind. I presume the idea is to guard against suicide.

After I have been thoroughly searched I clothe myself in the soiled old shirt and trousers, put on the felt shoes, throw the coat over my shoulder and take my cap in my hand. I can not, for the life of me, see what use can be made of a cap in a dark cell. Before I hand over my own trousers to the Captain I take my handkerchief out of the pocket.

"You can't have that," says the Captain gruffly; and he snatches the handkerchief out of my hand.

Well, of all the unbelievable stupidity!

Suicide again, I suppose. But has it never occurred to anyone responsible for this System that a man can strangle himself more easily with his undershirt or drawers than with his handkerchief?

Ah! I recall it now—the case of that poor fellow who committed suicide down in this place several years ago. It was with his handkerchief that he strangled himself; so I have been told.

The official remedy, therefore, for suicide in the punishment cells is to take away your handkerchief.

And then—leave you your underclothes.

In none too pleasant a frame of mind toward prison officialdom, I enter my iron cage. It is the first one of the eight and is absolutely empty of everything except a papier-mâché bucket. There is no seat, no bed, no mattress or bedding, no place to wash, no water to wash with, nothing—except the bucket. I presume I ought to be grateful even for that. But I wish it had a cover.

A convict trusty, who now appears within the radius of the electric light, hands me a round tin can, and the grated door is banged to and locked. I take my seat upon the floor and await developments.

Soon the trusty hands me, through an extra large slot in the door, a roll of pieces of newspaper, evidently intended for possible toilet purposes. There soon follows a slice of bread, and then there is poked through the slot the end of a long tin funnel which holds a precise measure of water. I hold my tin can to the end of the funnel and receive a gill—neither more nor less than exactly one gill—which is to last me through the night. I never appreciated before what a small quantity is measured by a gill. The water covers the bottom of my tin can to the depth of about an inch and a half.

And three gills of water is all the inmates of this place are allowed in twenty-four hours.

And up to the time that Warden Rattigan took office and first visited the jail, all the water a man here was allowed in twenty-four hours was one gill!

No wonder the men down here go insane! No wonder they commit suicide!

The electric light, held close to the grated door of my iron cage, has enabled me thus far to see the operations of Captain Martin and the trusty. Now they pass along to the other cells, and I can see nothing except the fragments of their moving shadows on the wall opposite. But they are stopping at the doors of the other cells, and are evidently giving out more bread and gills of water. So there must be other prisoners; I shall not be alone in the darkness, thank Heaven!

Having finished their duties, the trusty departs and the Captain follows; after extinguishing the electric light. The iron door turns on its hinges and is slammed shut; the key grates in the lock.

Standing up, with my hands and face close to the iron bars of the grated door, I can catch a glimpse of daylight at either end of the dungeon where the windows let in a small portion of the bright sunlight I left outside. I hear the Captain's heavy footfalls retreating along the stone passage toward his office; then, muffled by the distance and the heavy iron door already closed, the outer door clangs faintly to, and is more faintly locked.

Then a moment of deepest quiet. Only the incessant whirr, whirr, whirr, of the dynamo through the opposite wall; and that seems not so much like a noise as like a throbbing of the blood at my temples. The rest is silence.

The sound of a voice breaks the stillness.

"Number One! Hello, Number One!"

As my cell is nearest the door, doubtless I am Number One.

108

"Hello!" I rejoin.

"Where do you come from?"

"From the basket-shop."

"Say! Is that guy, Tom Osborne, workin' there yet?"

Gathering my wits together so as not to be taken unawares, I answer slowly, "Yes, he's working yet."

Then there comes a hearty, "Well, say! He's all right, ain't he? What's he doin' now?"

I hesitate for an instant as to how to answer this, but determine that frankness is the best course.

"He's talking to you."

"What!"

"He's talking to you."

"Gee! You don't mean to say that you're the guy?"

"Well, I'm Tom Brown; it's pretty much the same thing, you know."

"Well, say, Tom! You're a corker! I can't believe it's you!"

Here a gentle voice breaks in. "Yes, I guess it is all right. I thought I recognized his voice."

"Yes, I'm the fellow you mean," is my reassuring statement. I feel that things are opening well.

"Well, Tom! I'm Number Four, and that other fellow's Number Two. But, say, what're you in for?"

"I refused to work."

"Gee! Did you? How did you do it?"

So I tell the story again, of my complaint regarding our bad working material and the condition of my hands. Regarding the latter my statements, although somewhat exaggerated, are not so very far from the truth. As I mention my hands it occurs to me that they feel very disagreeably sticky. They must continue in that condition, however, for some time, for I can't wash them until I am out of this place.

My invisible audience listens apparently with interest to my story; and Number Four sums up his impressions with another enthusiastic, "Well, Tom, you're all right!" which seems to be his highest form of encomium.

Presently I take up some questioning on my own account.

"Hello, Number Four!" I begin.

A voice from the dim and fading daylight of the vault outside answers, "Hello, Tom!"

"How many fellows are there in here?"

"Six of us, now you've come. That fellow who spoke a while ago is in Two, next to you. There's a fellow in Three, but he's got a

109

bad cold so he can't talk very well. Then there's my partner in Five; and a big fellow in Eight, but he don't say much. Quite a nice party, you see, Tom. Glad you've come to join us. Say! how long are you goin' to be here?"

"I don't know. There was some talk of letting me out to-night if I would promise to behave myself."

Then the pleasant voice of Number Two breaks in again. "Well, if they don't let you out to-night, you're good till Monday, because they never let us out of here on Sunday."

I shall not attempt to reproduce all the conversation of this memorable night. It was about four o'clock in the afternoon when I entered the dark cell. During the next three hours, as I sat on the floor close to the door of my iron cage, our talk covered a wide range of topics from grave to gay. We touched upon almost every subject, from prison fare and the ethics of the jail to the comparative merits of various trans-Atlantic liners. We discussed politics—New York City, state and national; Prison Reform, from various angles; the character and conduct of celebrities we had seen or known—both in and out of prison; and other things too numerous to mention. I must confess that, on the whole, more intelligent, instructive, and entertaining conversation it has seldom been my lot to enjoy. I soon came to the conclusion that under favorable conditions the jail was decidedly the most sociable place in prison.

The brunt of the talk fell upon Number Four, Number Two and myself; with occasional remarks from Number Five. Number Three was not in condition to speak, as will be seen later, and he and Number Eight contributed only one remark apiece during the entire night. The leader of the party was Number Four, and I hate to think what we should have done without him.

So much for the lighter side of the matter. But all the time our conversation was going on, more and more the influence of the place kept closing in upon me; more and more I found myself getting into a state of helpless anger against the Prison System, the men who have been responsible for its continuance, and the stupid indifference of society at large in permitting it. The handkerchief performance seemed a fair example of the unreasoning, futile, incredible imbecility of the whole theory and practice.

The mention of the handkerchief reminds me of one of Number Four's early remarks.

"Hey, Tom, did you know a fellow committed suicide in your cell once?"

"No, did he?" I reply, feigning ignorance and yawning. "Well, I hope his ghost won't come around to-night! There isn't room for

110

two in this cell." At which frivolous remark they laugh. But in spite of my answer I do not feel in the least like laughing myself. The thought that I am locked into the very cell which was the scene of the tragedy of that poor human soul, whom a little decent treatment and kindly sympathy might perhaps have saved, only adds fuel to the flame of my wrath.

Before proceeding it may be well to give a brief account of my fellow-sufferers, as I became acquainted with them through the night or learned about them afterward. And let me begin by saying that I had fully expected that now at last I was to meet the worst that humanity has to show. While I had come to prison strongly inclined to disbelieve in the existence of a criminal class, as distinct from the rest of mankind, yet I had come with an open mind, ready to receive the facts as I found them, and duly readjust my previous opinions. I was entirely prepared to encounter many depraved and hardened men, but so far I had met none whom I thought hopelessly bad—quite the contrary. I had been put to work with the "toughest bunch of fellows in the prison"; and I had found myself side by side with Harley Stuhlmiller, and Jack Bell, and Blackie Laflam, and Patsy Mooney—the genial "baseball shark," and the "dime-novel Kid," who wanted to give me his grapes; to say nothing of that best of partners—Jack Murphy.

But surely in the jail, so I reasoned, I shall meet the "confirmed criminal." In this prison are fourteen hundred convicts—men who, under the law, have been found guilty of robbery, arson, forgery, murder—all kinds of crime; men condemned to live apart from the rest of mankind, to be caged within walls. And now in the jail—in this place of punishment of last resort—here where the refuse of the System is gathered, I must certainly come in contact with the vilest and most hopeless. Men who will submit to no law, no control—men without faith in God or man—men who even in prison will still pursue their violent and evil ways; now I shall get to know what such creatures are like.

And this is what I find.

Farthest away, at the other end of the row of iron cells, is Number Eight. He is a big, good-natured, husky chap from the enamel-shop; sent down to this place of supreme punishment because he had talked back to one of the citizen instructors. For what reason he is placed in Cell Eight, which has no wooden floor, so that its occupant has to lie on the bare iron plates covered with rivets, I am unable to state. Formerly none of these cells had wooden floors, and everyone slept on the rivets, rolling over and over through the night as each position in turn became unbearable.

111

Cells Seven and Six are empty.

In Cell Four is my sociable friend, whose name I learn is Joe; and in Cell Five is the man he referred to as his partner, with whom Joe was having a friendly little scrap when they were interrupted and sent down here. The two fellows are, apparently, on perfectly good terms, but Number Five thought Joe had done something, which Joe hadn't; so he punched Joe, and Joe punched him back. It was nothing more than a slight breach of discipline, for which a minimum punishment should have been inflicted—if anything more than a separation and a word of caution were necessary.

In Cell Three is the fellow with a bad cold. He is being punished for hitting another inmate over the head with a crowbar. This sounds rather serious, but the other fellow had called him an ugly name—a name which any man considers himself justified in resenting; and one effect of confinement being to make tempers highly inflammable, Number Three had resented the epithet with the nearest weapon handy.

In such cases there is no proper examination made to see if there are extenuating circumstances; little or no opportunity is given the prisoner to state his side of the case; no belief when he is allowed to state it. The convict is reported by an officer. That is enough; down he comes immediately.

Called upon in the course of the night by Joe to give an account of himself, Number Three makes his one remark. "You fellows'll hev to excuze be; I god such a cold id by 'ead I cad't talk. Besides I shouted so las' dight that I cudd't talk butch eddy how!"

I find myself wondering how Number Three manages to do without a handkerchief—having so bad a cold in the head. Blows his nose on his shirt, I suppose. Quite pleasant and cleanly for the next fellow who is to wear the shirt, and for whom it will not be washed by order of the Warden. Again I am thankful for that particular special privilege.

Now I come to Number Two, and, my feelings on this subject being rather strong, I shall not trust myself to do more than state coldly the plain facts. This boy, for he is only twenty-one years of age, on Tuesday of this week after being two weeks in the hospital, had an operation on his ear, being already deaf in that ear from an injury received before he came to prison. The operation was on Tuesday; on Thursday afternoon, two days later, he was discharged from the hospital as being able to work, although the wound in his ear had not yet healed. Being a slight, lightly-built youth, and just out of the hospital after an operation, he was put to work at—shoveling coal! But the next morning, Friday, before he had fairly

112

started on his job, he was ordered to the jail office. There he found that a report had come down from the hospital to the effect that while there he had been somewhat troublesome and had talked with another patient.

For this offense the sick lad was sent down here to the dark cell on bread and three gills of water a day. No handkerchief to wipe the running wound in his ear. No water to wash his ear or his face. Clad in filthy clothes. And when I arrived on Saturday afternoon he had been down here nearly thirty-six hours. And was due to stay at least thirty-six more, for "they never let us out of here on Sunday."

Nor is that all. This inhuman treatment—I hope I am not guilty of too much rhetoric in the use of the adjective—this punishment of being sent here to the dark cells, is only one, as I learn from my new friends, of five simultaneous punishments, all for the same offense.

There is First: Your imprisonment in the jail, under such conditions as I am trying to describe.

Second: Your hard-gained earnings are taken away by a fine which is charged against you on the prison books. As an instance, take my own case. My six days' work in the basket-shop would have entitled me, as a convict, to receive from the state of New York the munificent sum of nine cents. But my fine for spending one night in the punishment cells was fifty cents. So at the end of my week's work I owed the state of New York forty-one cents. If I had been a regular convict I should have had to work four weeks more before I could have got back even again. But, on the other hand, had I been a regular convict I should have been much more heavily fined, and my punishment would not have ended with a single night.

This is of course the highly humorous aspect of my particular case. To a prisoner who sometimes loses several years' pay for the privilege of spending a few days in these cells, there is precious little humor about it. At the mere whim of a bad-tempered keeper he may lose the acquisition of months of patient toil. And against the keeper there is no practicable appeal whatever, for the P. K. simply registers the action of the officers, on the theory that "discipline must be maintained." Experience has taught the convict that there is no use in kicking—that would only be to get into deeper trouble; so he takes his medicine as the shortest and quickest way out. But we may be quite sure that the convict does not forget his grievance, and ultimately Society pays the penalty.

But let us go on with the other punishments involved in this jail sentence.

Third: The disc upon your sleeve is bulls-eyed—that is,

113

changed to a circle—or taken off altogether, as a mark of disgrace. And you never can regain your disc, no matter how perfect your future conduct. Your sleeve shows to every observer that you have been punished; that you are or have been a disturbing, if not dangerous, character. It is astonishing how much the prisoners get to care about this disc, and how deeply they feel the disgrace implied in the loss of it. But however strange it seems, there can be no doubt as to the fact.

Fourth: If you have been fortunate enough to earn by a year's perfect record a good conduct bar upon your sleeve, that bar is taken away, or whatever credits you have gained toward a bar; and you have to begin your struggle all over again. Here also, however odd it may seem to us, the prisoners treasure greatly these evidences of a good record, and resent their loss.

Fifth: Some portion, if not all, of the commutation time which you may have gained by previous good conduct is also forfeited, so that you may have to serve out your full term.

Of course one can easily comprehend how this avalanche of punishments, all for the same offense, no matter how trivial, is admirably calculated to inspire in the prisoner respect for authority, loyalty to the state, and love for its officials. Its admirable reformatory influence must be apparent upon the slightest consideration.

Such were my companions of the dark cells, and such the nature of their offenses and punishments. These were the voices and personalities which came through the bars of my iron cage, reflected from the opposite wall.

It is a very curious experience—getting suddenly upon an intimate footing with a number of people whom you cannot see, acquainted only with their voices. The vaulted room gives each sound with peculiar distinctness, but I cannot tell where any voice comes from; they all sound equally near—equally far off. It is the same strange effect I noticed in my regular cell in the north wing. And as I think of that cell it seems by contrast rather homelike and pleasant, but very far away. I feel as if I had been in this place a large part of my natural life. At any rate I ought to be getting out before very long. And that reminds me——

"Hello, Number Four!" I call out. "Wasn't there another fellow here, a chap named Lavinsky, who was brought down on Wednesday evening?"

"Sure there was," answers the voice of Number Four. "They took him away about an hour before you came."

"What sort of a fellow was he?"

"Oh, he was a bug, all right. Threw his bread out of his cell and his water all over, and hollered a good deal. I guess they knew you was comin', didn't they? That's the reason they took him out. And, say! What do you think they wanted to do with Abey and me?" he continues. "They took us over to the north wing and wanted to put us in a couple of those screen cells. But nix for us! We refused to go into 'em. Said that Superintendent Riley had ordered those cells stopped, and they wasn't legal. Then Captain Martin sort of laughed and brought us over here. Seems as if they didn't want you to make our acquaintance, don't it?"

And it certainly does seem that way. [15]

On the whole, thanks to my agreeable companions, the time has passed so quickly that I am rather surprised when I hear the farther door unlocked and opened and steps coming along the passage. This must be Grant arriving to set me free. Now I must settle in my mind a question which has been troubling me for the last hour or so. Shall I go back to my cell or shall I spend the night down here?

On the one hand, is my rising anger and horror of the place, the evil influence of which I begin to feel both in body and in mind; on the other hand is the sense that I am nearer the heart of this Prison Problem than I have yet been; nearer, I believe, than any outsider has ever come. I am in the midst of an experience I can never have again, and it is what I came to prison to get. Moreover, if I go now, will there not arise a feeling among the men that at the last moment I failed to make good, that my courage gave out just at the end?

The steps reach the inner door. Which shall it be?

The key grates in the lock, I hear the inner door swing open, the electric light is turned on. Amid complete silence from the other cells my door is unlocked; and there appears before my astonished eyes no less a person than the P. K. himself, attended by another officer.

---

[15] I have been told, on very good authority, that it was seriously debated whether all the prisoners should not be removed from the jail before my arrival and stored elsewhere temporarily. But one of the trusties pointed out to a certain officer high in authority that it would be rather awkward if I heard of it, as I was almost sure to do; and thus in the end it would have a worse result than if things were allowed to drift. This view carried the day, so that the removal of Lavinsky was the only change made. The effort to place the two fellows in the screen cells, upon which Captain Martin was too wise to insist, was by Number Four's shrewdness defeated.

In an instant my mind is made up about one thing—I will not go with the P. K. anywhere. At the sight of his uniform a fierce anger suddenly blazes up within me and then I turn cold. All my gorge rises. Not at the man, for I certainly have no personal grievance against Captain Patterson, but at the official representative of this hideous, imbecile, soul-destroying System. I am seized by a mild fit of that lunatic obstinacy which I have once or twice seen glaring out of the eyes of men interviewed by the Warden down here; the obstinacy that has often in the course of history caused men to die of hunger and thirst in their cages of stone or iron, rather than gain freedom by submission to injustice or tyranny.

It is all very well to talk of breaking a man's spirit. It can be done; it has been done many times, I fear, in this and similar places of torture. But after you have thoroughly mastered his manhood by brutality—after you have violated the inner sanctuary of the divine spirit which abides in every man, however degraded—what then? What has become of the man? The poor, crushed and broken wrecks of humanity, shattered by stupid and brutal methods of punishment, which lie stranded in this and other prisons, give the answer.

I fear that in consequence of my somewhat disordered feelings I am lacking in proper respect for lawful authority. Instead of rising to greet the P. K. I remain seated on the floor in my old soiled and ragged garments, looking up at him without making a motion to shift my position. He is evidently surprised at my attitude, or my lack of attitude. Bending forward into my cell he whispers, "It's seven o'clock."

"Yes; thank you, sir." I am glad to find that I can still utter polite words, although I am seething within and remain doggedly obstinate in my seat on the floor. "But I think I will wait until Mr. Grant comes."

The P. K. seems surprised. With considerable difficulty he bends farther forward and whispers still more forcibly, "But it's seven o'clock, and you were to be let out at seven—it was all arranged."

"Yes, P. K.," I say, "and it's very kind of you to take all this trouble, but I don't quite know yet whether I want to go out. You see there are a lot of other fellows here, and——" I come to a stop, for I despair of being able to make the P. K. understand. And when one comes to think of it, I don't know of any reason why he should be expected to understand. I suppose it's the first time in his experience that a man in his senses has ever deliberately refused to be released from this accursed hole.

116

"It was all arranged that you were to come out now," insists the astonished P. K., getting more and more serious and perturbed. I shouldn't wonder if he thinks I've gone bughouse.

"Yes, but Mr. Grant was to come for me, and he——"

"Well, Mr. Grant told me to come for you, and it's all right," urges the anxious official.

I look up at him with what must be a tolerably obstinate expression of countenance. "I don't want to leave at present," I remark quietly, "and I shall stay here until Mr. Grant comes."

The P. K. looks at me for a moment as if he would like to order his attendant officer to haul me out by the scruff of the neck. Then he shakes his head in a hopeless fashion, and without another word bangs to and locks the grated door. The light is extinguished, and we hear the inner door shut and locked; footsteps resound faintly along the stone corridor, and the outer door is shut and locked.

"Hello, Tom!" This from Number Four.

"Hello!"

"Who was that? What did they want?"

"It was the P. K. He came to let me out."

"Come to let you out; and you didn't go? Gee! I wish they'd try it on me. What did you tell 'em?"

"I told the P. K. that I would wait until Grant came. I told him I hadn't had enough of the jail yet." At this delirious joke there is laughter loud and long. Then Number Four says,

"Ah, don't go, Tom! We need you down here!"

"That's so. Sure we do!" chimes in the voice of Number Two.

And then there is a murmur of assent along the line.

"Well, boys," I say, "I'll see about it. I shouldn't have any supper now if I did go out, and I suppose this floor is as soft as any pine planks I've ever slept on. But if I am to stay, we must get better acquainted."

"Sure!" sings out Number Four. "Let's all tell what we would like for supper. What do you say, boys, to a nice, juicy beefsteak with fried potatoes?"

At this there is a general howl of jovial protest; loudest of all the poor lad in Cell Two, who has had nothing but bread and water for thirty-six hours, and who, to emphasize the fact of his coming from Boston, says something humorous about beans. The way these prisoners can joke in the face of their sufferings and privations has been a continual wonder to me.

It is not long before our talk turns in a new direction. The popularity of the prison officials is discussed. They all agree that the present Superintendent of Prisons is all right; that Warden Rattigan is square; and not only tends to his business but is on the level. Joe from Cell Four expresses his opinion that the treatment by the prisoners of the Warden when he first took office last summer was inexcusable. "That strike was a dirty deal," he says. I am glad to hear about this, and Joe goes on to give me some interesting details. It was not due to the poor food, he declares, although that was the supposed cause. In reality, he assures me, the strike was instigated by some of the officers who had no use for Rattigan. They spread all manner of stories against him before he was appointed, and after he took office they deliberately egged on the convict ringleaders to strike and fairly pushed the men into it. This tallies with certain inside information I had at the time of the strike so I am not indisposed to believe it.

As we are still discussing these interesting matters, once more the faint sound of a key turning in a lock is heard and the opening of the outer door. This surely must be Grant. Steps come along the passage, and Joe makes a final appeal. "Say, don't go, don't go!" he whispers at the last moment. "Stick it out, Tom! Stick it out!"

That settles it. I remain. Joe has won the day, or at least the night.

The key turns in the inner lock and we hear the door turn on its hinges. Then the light is lighted, the grated door of my cell is again thrown open, and Grant stands there. This time I rise. "Come in here," I say, "where we can't be heard," and taking him by the arm I lead him back into the darkness of the cell.

"What's the matter?" asks Grant, with a trace of some anxiety in his tone.

"Nothing's the matter," I answer. "Only I'm learning such a lot down here that I ought to stay the night. There are four or five fellows in the other cells and I can't afford to miss the opportunity. Just explain to the P. K., will you? I'm afraid I was rather rude to him."

Grant explodes in mirth. "Well, you did jar him a little. He telephoned up to my house while I was at supper and said, 'Please hurry down here, for I can't get that fellow out!'"

I can not help laughing myself at the poor P. K.—panic-stricken because a man refused to come out of the jail. "Now let me stay the night here," I say to Grant, "and send someone for me at six o'clock to-morrow morning. But for Heaven's sake don't make it any later than six," I add.

Grant is a little anxious, feeling his responsibility to the Warden. "Are you sure you'd better do this?" he asks. "How do you feel? How are you standing it?"

118

"Oh, it's the most interesting thing I have done yet," I answer, "and my experience would have been a failure without it. Now, don't worry. I shall last until six o'clock in the morning at any rate. But remember—not a minute later than six!"

Grant promises to arrange it, and our whispered conference comes to an end. He and the other officer take their departure; again the inner door is shut and locked, the footsteps travel down the corridor, the outer door is shut and locked; and then silence, which is broken once more by the voice of Number Four, an anxious voice this time.

"Has he gone?"

Silence. Then Number Two's gentle tones, "I think he went with the officer. I don't hear anything in his cell. Yes, he must have gone."

A sigh comes from Joe, and I think it unfair to let the matter go any farther. Some remarks might be made which would prove embarrassing.

"No, boys, I haven't deserted you!"

I shall not attempt to set down the words that follow.

Now I truly am a prisoner; I can not possibly get myself out of this iron cage, and there is no one to let me out. There is no one except my fellow prisoners within hearing, no matter how loud I might cry for help. This at any rate is the real thing, whatever can be said of the rest of my bit. And now that all chance of escape is gone I begin to feel more than before the pressure of the horror of this place; the close confinement, the bad air, the terrible darkness, the bodily discomforts, the uncleanness, the lack of water. My throat is parched, but I dare not drink more than a sip at a time, for my one gill—what is left of it—must last until morning. And then there is the constant whirr-whirr-whirring of the dynamo next door, and the death chamber at our backs.

For a while after the departure of Grant we are still talkative. There is a proposition to settle down for the night, but Joe scouts the notion. So the conversation is continued; and by way of reviving our drooping spirits Joe asks again, "Say, fellows! What would you say now to a nice, thick, juicy steak with fried potatoes?"

As by this time we are all ravenously hungry and some of us well-nigh famished, what is said to Joe will not bear repetition.

Then we have music. Joe sings an excellent rag-time ditty. Number Two follows with the Toreador's song from "Carmen," sung in a sweet, true, light tenor voice that shows real love and appreciation of music. I too am pressed to sing, but out of consideration for my fellow prisoners decline, endeavoring in other

119

ways to contribute my share to the sociability of the occasion. I can at any rate be an appreciative listener.

After a time, announcing my intention of going to sleep, I stretch out full length on the hard floor—and it certainly is hard. However, it will not be the first time I've spent a night on the bare boards; although I've never done so in a suicide's cell, with the death chamber close at hand. I don't wonder men go crazy in these cells; that dynamo, with its single insistent note, slowly but surely boring its way into one's brain, is enough to send anyone out of his mind, even if there were no other cause.

This is the place where I had expected to meet the violent and dangerous criminals; but what do I find? A genial young Irishman, as pleasant company as I have ever encountered, and a sweet-voiced boy singing "Carmen."

Is this Prison System anything but organized lunacy? I fail to see where ordinary common sense or a single lesson of human experience has been utilized in its development.

"Are you asleep yet, Tom?" It is Joe's voice again.

"No, not yet."

"Well, you know, we don't do much of that down here; but it's a mighty sociable place." Then, as if the idea of sociability had suggested it, "Any bedbugs yet?"

Horrors!

"Bedbugs!" I gasp, then laugh at the suggestion. "I don't see any bed; how can there be any bedbugs?"

"Well, I guess you'll have plenty visiting you before the night's over," says Joe.

Number Two's plaintive voice is heard again, "I've just killed two."

Good Lord! it only needed this!

Immediately I begin to feel myself attacked by vermin from all directions. I know of no other instance where the power of suggestion can give so much discomfort. Once mention vermin, and all repose of mind is gone for me until I can reach a bathtub. Just at present, however, I should feel grateful if I could even wash my hands.

Stretched on the floor at the back of the cell I try to find a comfortable position, but without success. I toss and turn on the hard boards, and finally give a groan of discouragement.

"What's the matter, Tom?" Number Four is alert as usual.

"Oh, nothing, only I can't find a soft spot in this confounded place. It wouldn't be so bad if I had a pillow."

"Guess you don't know how to sleep on the floor," says Joe,

and he proceeds to give useful instructions as to the best means of arriving at a minimum of discomfort. Following Joe's advice, I remove my felt shoes, and with my shirt rolled up on top of them have a very fair pillow. My coat must be taken off and thrown over the body as a coverlet, for one gets more warmth and comfort in this way than when it is worn. As I make these changes I also shift my place in the cell, moving over toward the door; for just as Joe is giving me his suggestions, a suspicious crawling on my neck gives the chance to remove a large-sized bedbug which, in spite of the special cleaning the cell had undergone just before my arrival, has found its way in.

And now comes a weird episode of this strange night's experience. What the hour is I can only guess; but, having heard the distant sounds of the nine o'clock train going west, and the nine-fifty going east, I think it must be in the neighborhood of half past ten. Lying on the hard floor I am feeling not sleepy, but very tired—drowsy from sheer mental exhaustion. I hear my name called again, asking if I am still awake, but I do not answer, for I hardly know whether I am or not.

Suddenly a wail comes from the next cell, "Oh, my God! I've tipped over my water!"

For an instant I feel as if I must make an attempt to batter down the iron wall between us. I have been hoarding my own water; let me share it with that poor sick boy. But the next thought brings me to my senses. I am powerless. I can only listen to the poor fellow's groans, while tears of rage and sympathy are wiped from my eyes on the sleeve of my soiled and ragged shirt.

"How did it happen?" I hear Joe ask.

"Oh, I just turned over and stretched my legs out and kicked the can over. And now—I can't get any water until to-morrow morning! Oh, what in Hell shall I do?"

The speaker's voice dies away into inarticulate moaning. Quietly I reach over for my own precious can of water and place it securely in a corner—far removed from any probable activities of my feet. Then presently as I lie quietly, awake and listening, I become aware of a terrible thing. I hear Number Two talking to himself and then calling out to Joe, "When he comes in here to-morrow morning, I'll just—I'll—I'll throw my bucket at his head!" and I realize that he is talking of an assault upon the keeper. Then he begins to mutter wild nothings to himself. Gradually there dawns upon me a hideous thought—the poor lad is going out of his mind.

What shall I do? What can I do? What can anyone do? If we could only get some water to him! But the iron cage is solid on all

121

sides. If we could only arouse the keeper! But there is no possible way to make anyone hear. We could all scream our lungs out and no one would come. We might all go mad and die in our cells and no one would come.

But if I am helpless, not so Number Four. I soon hear Joe beginning to talk with the boy; and I perceive that Joe also has realized the situation, and with admirable patience and tact is applying the remedy. Never have I witnessed a finer act of Christian charity toward suffering humanity, never more skilful treatment of a sick and nervous fellow-creature. The first thing an intelligent doctor would advise in such a case is that the patient should confide in a sympathetic friend, air his grievance, get it out of his system, let the dangerous gases escape. A more sympathetic friend than Joe one could not find. Bit by bit he draws Number Two's story from him and encourages him to vent his anger at the prison officials and their whole infernal system, and in fact at all things and persons related to his present situation.

Then having laid bare the wound Joe begins to apply antiseptic and soothing treatment. "Now you mustn't worry too much about this thing," is the advice of the sympathetic listener. "You've had a rotten deal, but listen to this." And he relates some peculiarly atrocious case of punishment—true or otherwise. He gradually soothes the boy's irritated temper, and then at the appropriate moment says, "Now give us another song!"

Number Two, after some demur, complies; sings a tender, sentimental ballad, and evidently feels better.

Then Joe cracks a joke; chats with Number Two about a few topics of general interest; and then, yawning, expresses his own intention of going to sleep. There are a few scattered incidental remarks at ever longer intervals. Then as I listen carefully and hear nothing in the next cell, I conclude that Number Two is safely over the strain for the time; that with Joe's help he has conquered his black mood and is back on the right road again.

Good for you, Joe! Whatever your sins and failures of the past, whatever your failures and sins of the future, I do not believe that the Recording Angel will forget to jot down something to your credit for this night in Cell Four.

Quiet has settled upon us. There is heavy breathing in some of the cells, and I think that even Joe is contradicting his statement regarding sleep in the jail. But for a long time I can get no such relief. My ever increasing sympathy and anger are making me feverish. But at last, somewhere near midnight as near as I can judge, I do succeed in dropping off to sleep. It is a restless slumber at the best, for I am repeatedly made aware of some bone or muscle with the existence of which I am not usually concerned. So I twist and turn, as every few moments I am hazily and painfully aroused into semi-consciousness.

But even this restless slumber is denied me. Before I have found relief in it for more than half an hour I am suddenly and roughly awakened. The door of the cell is rattled violently and a harsh voice calls out, "Here! Answer to your name! Brown!"

Recovering my dazed and scattered senses as well as I can, I reply, "Here, sir!" and have a mind to add, "Still alive," but suppress the impulse as I wish to ask a favor.

"Officer," I say, as politely as possible, "that poor fellow in the next cell has tipped over his can of water. Can't you let him have some more?"

The answer is far more courteous than I deserve for such an unheard-of and scandalous proposition. The keeper says shortly and gruffly, "'Fraid I can't. 'Gainst the rules." And he coolly proceeds to wake up the occupants of the other cells.

Setting my teeth firmly together, while the blood goes rushing to my temples, I feel for the moment as if I should smother. Perhaps it is as well that I am under lock and key, for I should like to commit murder. To think that any man can grow so callous to human suffering as to forget the very first duty of humanity. Even soldiers on the battlefield will give a drink of water to a dying enemy. And here we have an organized System which in cold blood forbids the giving of a few drops to the parched lips of a sick lad, to save him from misery and madness! And if I am almost stifling with anger at the outrage, what must those men feel who are really suffering? What must those have felt who in the past have been kept here day after day, slowly dying of thirst or going mad on one gill of water in twenty-four hours?

Is it imagination that the very air here seems to be tainted with unseen but malign and potent influences, bred of the cruelty and suffering—the hatred and madness which these cells have harbored? If ever there were a spot haunted by spirits of evil, this must surely be the place. I have been shown through dungeons that seemed to reek with the misery and wretchedness with which some lawless medieval tyrant had filled them; but here is a dungeon where the tyrant is an unreasoning, unreachable System, based upon the law and tolerated by good, respectable, religious men and women. Even more then than the dungeons of Naples is this "the negation of God"; for its foundation is not the brutal whim of a degenerate despot, but the ignorance and indifference of a free and civilized people. Or rather, this is worse than a negation of God, it is a betrayal of God.

After duly waking my companions the keeper amuses himself by fussing with the steam pipes. The vault was already disagreeably close and hot; but he chooses to make it still hotter, and none of us dares to remonstrate. Then he turns out the light and goes his way, and he certainly carries with him my own hearty maledictions, if not those of my fellow prisoners.

It is hopeless to think of going to sleep again at once, although my head is thick and my eyes heavy with fatigue. So again I sit close to the grated door and open up communication with Joe. As usual, he is entirely willing to give his attention, and enters readily into conversation.

"Hey, Tom! Do you want to know my name? It's Joseph Matto. Funny name for an Irishman, ain't it? Well, you know, it ain't my real name. My real name's McNulty. But you see it was this way. When my case came up in court, down in New York, they called out, 'Joseph Matto'; and the cop said, 'Here, you, get up there!' I said, 'That ain't my name'; and he said, 'Never you mind, get up!' So you see I got some other fellow's name, but I thought I might as well keep it, and so I have ever since.

"But it's all right, because I don't want to disgrace my folks. They don't know where I am, and I wouldn't have my mother know for anything. You see, I'm the black sheep of the family, the rest are all right. I'm the only one that ain't goin' straight. But when I get out of here I mean to go straight. Say, Tom, do you think I can get a job, here in Auburn? My bit is up in December, and I should like to stay here and get straight before I go back home."

"When you get out," is my answer, "it will be up to me to stand treat for a dinner of beefsteak and fried potatoes, at any rate. And I'll do the best I can to help you get a job, Joe, if you really do mean to go straight. But in that neither I nor any one else can help you; you know you'll have to do that yourself."

Poor Number Four! I have not the slightest doubt he means what he says, but here again—this cursed System. It is particularly deadening to a young fellow like Joe. He evidently has just that lively, good-natured, shiftless, irresponsible temperament which needs to be carefully trained in the bearing of responsibility.

While Joe and I are conversing, Number Eight makes his one remark. "Would there be a job for a bricklayer around here?"

I don't know, and tell him so; but add, as in Joe's case, that if he means to go straight I will gladly do what I can for him; and in any event I consider that I owe each of them a good dinner. Thus it is agreed that they will all dine with me in turn upon the happy occasions of their release.

"By the way, Tom, did you go up to that Bertillon room?" Joe is off on a new tack.

"Oh, yes. I did all the regular stunts."

"Were you measured and photographed, and all that?"

"Yes, and my finger prints taken. I went through the whole thing."

"Gee! Well, then, they'll have your picture in the rogues' gallery, won't they, along with the rest of us?"

"I suppose they will," is my answer, and then I tell how my scars and marks were all discovered and duly set down in the record; and wind up with a variation of the same mild joke which so bored the clerk of the Bertillon room. "And do you know, boys, after he had got me all sized up and written down, I felt as if it would never be safe for me to adopt burglary as a profession; and I've always rather looked forward to that."

My companions are not bored but appreciative, they laugh with some heartiness. Then after a pause Joe says quite seriously, "Well say, Tom! I can just tell you one thing, you needn't ever have any fear that your house will be entered!"

"Oh! Do you think the crooks will all recognize me as one of themselves?"

"Sure!" is Joe's hearty rejoinder. He evidently considers it a compliment, and I accept it as such. At any rate I have apparently hit upon rather a novel form of burglary insurance.

It must be somewhere between half past one and two o'clock that sheer exhaustion sends me off to sleep again. This time my slumber is more successful than before. It is only occasionally that the discomfort of the hard floor forces me back into consciousness, and forces me also to such changes of position as seem necessary to prevent my bones coming through. Many of them seem to be getting painfully near the surface.

It was Number Five, I think, who informed me that it is the custom down here for the keeper to visit us every four hours—at half past twelve and half past four. The first visit I have described. After that, for nearly three hours, I get such sleep as the hard floor affords. About half past four I am having an interval of semi-consciousness—enough to realize dimly how utterly worn out I still feel both in body and mind, and how both crave more rest. So I am struggling very hard not to awake, when the light of the keeper's electric bull's-eye flashes through the iron grating straight into my eyes.

With curses too violent and sincere for utterance I report myself still in existence.

Now I am so constituted that at the best of times a sudden awakening always annoys me greatly. Just now it quite upsets my equilibrium. A torrent of rage and hate surges up through my whole being; it fairly frightens me by its violence. For a moment I feel as if I were being strangled. Then I make up my mind that I must and will get to sleep again, in spite of the keeper and his infernal light; and I make desperate attempts to do so, for I realize that I am expected to speak in chapel before many hours, and have a trying day before me. I am bound, therefore, to have myself in no worse condition than I can possibly help.

But of course it is impossible to get to sleep again, I can only follow my whirling thoughts. How in the world am I ever to speak to those men in chapel? What in Heaven's name can I say? How can I trust myself to say anything? How can I urge good conduct, when my whole soul cries out in revolt? How can I preach resignation and patience against this dark background of horror?

An aching, overwhelming sense of the hideous cruelty of the whole barbaric, brutal business sweeps over me; the feeling of moral, physical and mental outrage; the monumental imbecility of it all; the horrible darkness; the cruel iron walls at our backs; the nerve-racking monotone of the whirring dynamo through the other wall; the filth; the vermin; the bad air; the insufficient food; the denial of water; and the overpowering, sickening sense of accumulated misery—of madness and suicide, haunting the place. How can I speak of these things? How can I not speak of them? How can I——

Hark!

Click! Click! Click! Click! I hear the levers being pressed down by the officer, and the stirring of life along the galleries.

Click! Click! Click! Click! I had no idea it was possible to hear the sounds from the south wing, 'way in here. And it is still so early in the morning—only half past four.

Click! Click! Click! It must be the prisoners who work in the kitchens, they are the only ones who would be moving at such an hour. But again, how is it possible to hear them so far away, shut in as we are by stone walls and iron doors?

Uneasily I shift my position and turn over on my left side, which feels temporarily less bruised and painful than the other. The clicking stops. But other vague sounds succeed; and then suddenly——

126

Tramp! Tramp! Tramp! Tramp! It is the march of the gray companies down the stone walk of the yard.

Tramp! Tramp! Tramp! Tramp! It is certainly not only the kitchen gang, for there must be many companies of them.

Tramp! Tramp——

But this is ridiculous, at half past four in the morning! It can't be true, it must be my imagination. I am not really hearing these sounds, for my reason tells me they are impossible.

Nevertheless I do hear them. Tramp! Tramp! Tramp! Tramp!

I try in vain to reason myself out of the evidences of my senses. I am hearing sounds that I am sure do not exist.

Tramp! Tramp! Tramp——

Heavens! Am I going mad?

This is past bearing. I abandon the attempt to sleep and sit up. As I do so the cell is suddenly filled with flying sparks which dance from one end to the other. Aghast, I steady myself with my back against the side of the cell.

This is getting serious. I grit my teeth together, and, shutting my eyes in the hope of keeping out the sight of the flitting sparks, I say firmly to myself, "This must not be. Don't lose your nerve. Cool down. Control yourself. Slow up. Keep steady."

As I rise to my feet my head seems to clear, the sparks disappear, the sound of marching footsteps had already ceased. There is nothing to see or hear—only the dreadful blackness and the dead silence of the night. I take two turns about the cell, carefully refraining from kicking over the bucket in the corner, and then stand close to the grating, in the hope of a breath of cool, fresh air. But there is no such thing in this fœtid place.

"Joe! Are you awake?"

"Hello! What's the matter?"

"For God's sake talk to me!"

"Sure! What shall we talk about?"

"Anything. I don't care. Only something."

So Joe begins to chat with me, and presently Number Two joins in, and Number Five has a few words to say. What we talk about I have not the faintest recollection; it is the only part of this night's occurrences that makes no impression whatever on my memory. I only know that I am longing for speedy escape as I have seldom longed for anything; that I am saying constantly to myself, "It can't be more than an hour more! They must surely come in about forty minutes! Half an hour! Half an hour! It can't go beyond that! Oh, why don't they come?"

127

I answer any remarks directed to me quite at random, for I am waiting, waiting, waiting, and listening.

An hour and a half does not seem such an endless period of time usually. Well, it all depends. When you are in a dark prison cell, waiting for deliverance, it seems a lifetime. I lived through every hour in the minute of that interminable period of five thousand four hundred seconds.

At last I hear a sound—one of the most welcome sounds I ever heard—the six o'clock train blowing off steam over at the New York Central station. I find myself wondering why I am not ready to shout with joy, and I discover it is because I feel as if all power of emotion had been crushed out of me. It is not merely utter and hopeless fatigue; it is as if something had broken inside of me; as if I could never be joyous again; as if I must be haunted forever by a sense of shame and guilt for my own share of responsibility for this iniquitous place. My sensation, when at last I hear the sound of the key in the lock of the outer door, is not one of exultation, only of approaching relief from deadly pain—pain which has become almost insupportable.

Once more we hear the outer door open and steps coming along the passage. I rise from my seat on the floor, and put on my shirt and shoes as I whisper, "Good bye, boys. I wish I could take you with me." Then the inner door is opened, the light is lighted, and my cell door swings out.

Some one stands there—I do not know who—I do not care. Listlessly, like one in a dream, I pick up my cap and coat; and silently, wearily, move out and toward the bench where I changed my clothes last night. Last night!—a thousand years ago. The officer—the keeper—the man, whoever he is, who has come to release me, produces my regular prison uniform; and listlessly, silently, wearily, I make the change, dropping my jail garments upon the floor. I feel as if I should like to grind my heels into the loathsome, hated things.

With a parting look along the row of cells which imprison my comrades, and choking down my feelings as I think of the sick lad we are leaving without water, I stumble along the passage to the jail office, pausing only while my attendant locks behind us the two iron doors. Another moment and I feel my lungs expand with a deep refreshing breath, and find myself out in the ghostly quiet of the prison yard.

The morning air is fresh and cool, and there is a soft gray light which seems to touch soothingly the old gray stones of the prison; but I have a feeling as if nothing were alive, as if I were a gray, uneasy ghost visiting a city of the dead. The only thing suggestive of life seems to be the sound of my heavy shoes upon the stone pavement.

I have a remote impression that my attendant is saying something. Perhaps I answer him. I think I do, but I am not sure. If so, it is only from the force of habit, not from any conscious mental process.

We traverse the upper part of the yard and enter the main building. Here my shoes make such a clatter on the stone floor that my guide looks at them inquiringly. I do not know whether he recommends their removal or whether I do it of my own accord; I am only aware that I have taken them off and am carrying them in my left hand as we mount the iron stairs and creep quietly along the familiar gallery of the second tier.

At Number 15 we stop, the key is turned in the lock, the lever clicks, the door opens, and I enter my cell. I think the man says something; I do not know. I stand motionless just within the door, as it swings to and is locked. The footsteps of my guide retreat along the gallery, down the stairs, and so out of hearing.

There is no sound in the cell house. All is silent, as the gray light of morning steals through the barred windows into the corridor and through the grated door into my cell.

What next?

I do not know.

Suddenly there wells up within me a feeling which is no longer rage, it is a great resistless wave of sympathy for those poor fellows in that Hell I have just left; for those who have ever been there; for those in danger of going there; for all the inmates of this great city within the walls—this great community ruled by hate—where wickedness is the expected thing—where love is forbidden and cast out.

Obeying an impulse I could not control if I would, I throw myself on my knees, with my arms on the chair and my face in my hands, and pray to Our Father who art in Heaven.

My prayer is for wisdom, for courage, for strength. Wisdom to determine my duty, courage to endeavor, and strength to persevere.

May I be an instrument in Thy hands, O God, to help others to see the light, as Thou hast led me to see the light. And may no impatience, prejudice, or pride of opinion on my part hinder the service Thou hast given me to do.

CHAPTER XIV
SUNDAY—THE END

After the emotional crisis I have just passed through, I find myself quite unstrung. For nearly half an hour I can do nothing but sit, limp and exhausted, in the chair and give way to my feelings. On the whole, this is a relief, although it leaves me very weak and wretched. At length, the realization that I must soon take my place in line for the duties of the early morning pulls me together; and after pouring cool water from the meager supply in my pail over my head and face, rearranging my clothes, and draining to the bottom my tin drinking cup, I am somewhat refreshed. Looking out from my cell across the corridor and through the barred windows of the outer wall, I find the promise of a bright, sunny day; but it gives me no pleasure. I feel utterly dull and depressed. Only a few hours more and I shall be gone forever from this narrow cell—back to my own comfortable home; but the thought arouses no enthusiasm. It does not seem to matter much in the sum of things whether I go or stay. Nothing seems to matter much except the physical sufferings of those poor fellows down in the jail; and at the thought a bitter anger sweeps over me again.

After a few moments, however, I once more regain control of myself, and wait patiently at the door of the cell for the day's routine to begin.

Before long I hear in the corridor below the clicking of levers and the tread of marching feet. A shiver goes through me as I think of the last time I heard such sounds. But those were imaginary, these are real. Soon, bucket in hand, I am once more traversing the long gallery and falling in line with the rest of my company at the yard door. The prisoners whose faces I can see are eyeing me curiously, and in a vague way I am wondering whether I bear any outward marks of the jail. I feel as if I must have somewhere upon me an unmistakable stamp of it, which may be a disfigurement for the rest of my life.

Sharply the Captain gives the signal and we set off on our march down the yard. I know it is sunny, for I can see the shadows of the trees upon the ground, but all things look unfamiliar and unreal. I go through the usual motions, but I am not thinking of what I am doing, or of anything else, for that matter. Everything seems cold, lifeless, dead. Yet I am conscious of making an effort to do my duty cheerfully. I have a curious feeling of being two people at once. One going through the regular routine, and the other watching him as he does it.

One of my selves seems to be at a distance looking at the other self as he marches down the yard, empties his bucket at the sewage disposal building, and then, without pausing at the stands, marches up the yard again. There was a gleam of satisfaction in my passive self at the thought that my active self was going to leave the bucket behind, and that I should never see it again. But that mild pleasure is denied me. Of course on Sunday the buckets are needed in the cells, as the men are locked up after chapel services for the rest of the day. I had not thought of that.

On our way back I seem to be saying to myself, "You poor fellow! If you were not so dead tired, you'd march better." And then I feel rather indignant at myself for the criticism.

Arrived back in my cell, it seems to occur vaguely to one of my two selves—I do not know which—that there is something I have to do to-day. Breakfast of course. But after that—Oh, yes—the chapel. I am expected to speak. I shake my head and shut my eyes, feeling ill at the thought. To speak! I feel upon my lips the ghost of a smile at the bare notion. How absurd for any one to think I could do such a thing!

Nevertheless something must be done. I ought to send word to the Chaplain that I can't speak. How can I send it? I cannot think. Somehow the idea of blue floats across my mind. Oh, yes! Roger Landry and his blue shirt. I'll ask Landry to get word to the Chaplain.

Click! Click! Click! Again the levers start. Still in a sort of a daze I open my door, fall in line behind Jack Bell, join Landry farther along the gallery, descend the iron stairs and march to the mess-hall. Here the regular weekday arrangements are changed. For some reason, instead of turning to the right as usual, we go to the left and occupy seats in quite a different part of the hall—on the left of the center aisle and much farther back. The change makes me feel vaguely uncomfortable.

I don't know what there is for breakfast. I believe that I have eaten something or other, although I am sure I have not sampled the bootleg. I wish I could share my breakfast—such as it is—with those poor fellows in the jail. I wonder if Number Two has any water yet. But I mustn't think of that.

Returned from breakfast, Landry comes to my cell to express his interest and sympathy; for he once had his own dose of the jail. I wonder if his spirit was broken. I forget to ask him to do my errand to the Chaplain. I fear it is too late now. Perhaps I can find some

131

way to do it after I reach the assembly room; perhaps I can, when called upon, explain briefly that I am unable to speak; or perhaps after all it would be better to bluff it out the best way I can, and let it go at that.

After this decision I feel somewhat better. Turning to the locker, I find a piece of paper with the few notes I scrawled yesterday noon. I had expected to revise and arrange them this morning. I may as well try to fix the thing up somehow. But I can do nothing but stare helplessly at the paper; my brain refuses to work. My stupidity finally annoys me so much that I shove the piece of paper into my pocket, and make up my mind not to bother any more about the matter.

One or two of the trusties, passing along the gallery, stop to chat. They all seem to look at me as one might at a person who has been restored to life from the dead. I'm sure I feel so. I have always wondered how Dante must have felt after he had visited the Inferno. I think I know now.

There are footsteps along the corridors and galleries; it is the noise made by good Catholics returning from Mass. It seems that I could have gone myself had I known of the service. I am sorry I did not; perhaps it would have helped me to forget.

Soon the summons to chapel comes, and in single file we march upstairs and into the large assembly room, which is on the second story, immediately above the mess-hall. Here our company has seats on the right of the main aisle about two-thirds of the way to the platform. Row after row of men take their seats, until the large room is entirely filled with silent, motionless, gray figures. I do not see those sitting behind, I only hear them, for like the rest I stare straight in front of me.

Then I hear the sound of hand-clapping; and when I can see without turning my head, I join in the applause that greets the Chaplain and an organist and quartet of singers from one of the Auburn churches. As some of them are my personal friends, I can not help wishing that they had not chosen this particular Sunday to sing here.

In vain I try to fasten my attention upon the service, I can only follow my own thoughts. It is but one short week since I occupied a seat upon that same platform, and that short week has altered the whole tenor of my life. It can never be the same again that it has been. Whether I wish it or not, a bond of union has been forged between these men and me which can never be broken. I have actually lived their life, even if for only a short period of time; I have been made one of the gray brotherhood—for they have received me

132

as a brother; and I have realized their sufferings because in a very small degree I have shared them.

But at the present moment what am I to do? When I am called up to the platform, as I soon shall be, what shall I say to these men? I must not speak of the jail; but how can I help speaking of it? It is the one thing that just now dominates my mind.

The singing is beautiful and restful. I could enjoy it were it not for this terrible feeling of oppression at my head and heart. Finally the critical moment arrives. The Chaplain advances to the front of the stage.

"At this point in the service," he says, "we are to have something of a departure from the usual order of exercises. Last Sunday you listened to an address which the Honorable Thomas Mott Osborne came here to give you. To-day we are going to invite someone from your midst to speak."

The Chaplain pauses, then clears his throat and says, "We have with us here to-day a man who calls himself Thomas Brown."

With a startling suddenness that seems to threaten the roof comes a terrific explosion of hand-clapping, sounding, as a visitor afterwards described it, like a million of fire crackers. I feel my backbone tingling from end to end. At the same time I have an almost irresistible desire to get away somewhere and hide myself from all those eyes.

The Chaplain continues:

"His number is 33,333x."

For some reason or other this excites the sense of humor which lies so near the surface here, and loud laughter interrupts the speaker.

"I will ask Thomas Brown to come to the platform."

With my hands on the back of the bench in front, I pull myself up onto my feet; and when the men see me rise their frantic hand-clapping begins again. As I leave my seat and gain the central aisle, the whole room seems to rock back and forth. I walk to the front and mount the platform. As I do so, the Chaplain, the singers and others sitting there rise and join in the applause. I am absurdly, but momentarily, conscious of my prison clothes—the rough cotton shirt, gray trousers and heavy shoes, as I bow to the people on the stage and then face the audience.

The applause subsides and every face turns towards me expectantly. Oh, for the gift of the tongues of men and of angels! What an opportunity lies here before me! And I feel helpless to take advantage of it.

As I stand for a moment looking over the large audience,

feeling unable to make a start, my attention is arrested by the face of one of my gray brothers. He is an old man, I do not know him, I am not conscious of ever having seen him before, but the tears are rolling down his cheeks as he sits looking up at me.

Then as if a cloud were lifted from my spirit, I suddenly understand what it all means. These men are not seeing me, they are looking at Tom Brown—the embodied spirit of the world's sympathy. They have felt the sternness of society—the rigor of its law, the iron hand of its discipline. But now at this moment many of these men are realizing for the first time that outside the walls are those who care.

I said to these men last Sunday that I should try to "break down the barriers between my soul and the souls of my brothers." It was necessary so to endeavor in order to understand the conditions I came to study. But what has happened is that these men have broken down their own barriers; they have opened their hearts; they have dignified and ennobled my errand; they have transformed my personal quest for knowledge into a vital message from the great heart of humanity in the outside world—a heart that, in spite of all that is said and done to the contrary, beats in sympathy with all genuine sorrow, with all honest endeavor for righteousness.

Thrilling with this revelation of the true meaning of my own mission, lifted out of apathy and discouragement, I make my speech; but, alas, the words come haltingly and reflect but little of the warmth and exhilaration in my heart.

When the Chaplain spoke to me about saying a few words to you this morning—words of farewell, because here for a time at least we must separate—I did not realize that it was going to be so hard. Probably I am the only man, in all the years since this prison was built, to leave these walls with regret.

It is not necessary to give every word of my utterly inadequate address. I was in no physical or mental condition to speak; my audience was almost too moved to hear. From a mere reading of the words that fell from my lips no one would understand the situation. But the prisoners understood; they listened with emotions which few can appreciate to my words of greeting and farewell and my prophecy of the new day soon to dawn for them.

First I spoke of the value of my experience to the Commission on Prison Reform as well as to me personally, for I knew that they had seen the doubts expressed in many of the newspapers as to the usefulness of my "experiment." I thanked the officers for their coöperation, and the prisoners for the way they had received me.

I must confess that I was unprepared for the way in which you men have carried out your part of the bargain. I consider that the restraint, courtesy, and loyalty to me and to my experiment have been very wonderful, and never shall I forget it. There has not been a word or look from beginning to end that I would have had otherwise. You have received me exactly as I asked you to—as one of yourselves.

I believed that a wide popular interest had been aroused, which could not help working for good.

In fact, with the aid of our friends the newspapers, we have had considerable advertising this last week, you and I. The personal part of this advertising I do not like—it would be pleasant if I could know that I should never again see my name in the newspapers—but doubtless it all works out for good in the long run. Certainly in this case I believe that more people have been thinking about the Prison System in New York State within the last week than any week since Auburn Prison was built; and while much of that interest will of course evaporate, for we need not expect the millennium yet awhile, nevertheless the ground has been tilled for the work that is to come.

Then I dwelt upon the tasks which lay before us to do—before them and before me. It was my task to go out in the world and help in the fight against human servitude in the prisons, but they had a much harder task.

Your part is the most important of all. It is just to do your plain duty here, day by day, in the same routine; but accepting each new thing as it comes along and striving to make of that new thing a success. Men, it is you alone who must do it. Nobody else can.

So then give to the Warden and to all the officers your hearty support; aid in the endeavor to make this institution all that it should be, all that it can be.

An old poet, Sir Richard Lovelace, once wrote:
"Stone walls do not a prison make,
Nor iron bars a cage."

135

Last night perhaps I should not have altogether agreed with Sir Richard; but of course what he meant was that, in spite of all the bolts and bars which men can forge, the spirit is always free; that you cannot imprison. In spite of your own confinement here you possess after all the only true liberty that there is to be found anywhere—the freedom of the spirit; the liberty to make yourselves new men, advancing day by day toward the strength and the courage and the faith which when you go out from these walls will enable you to lead such a life that you will never come back.

In explaining why I could not go into particulars regarding any conclusions I may have reached as to the Prison System, I realized that I was on delicate ground. I was sorely tempted to relate some of my last night's experiences in the jail, but I felt that were I to do so there was no telling what the result might be. The men were strangely moved by the whole situation, and I had the feeling that the room contained a great deal of explosive material that a chance spark might ignite. So I bit my lips, and forced myself away from the dangerous topic.

The time has not yet come for a statement of any particular conclusions or ideas. My experience is so new—particularly some of it—that I can hardly be expected just now to see things in their right relations. If I were to let myself go and state exactly what I do think at the present moment, I might say some things I should regret later. So it is better to wait and allow the experience to settle in my mind; and as I get farther away from it, things will assume their right proportions.

Reiterating my belief in the value of the experiment, I drew to a conclusion.

The time has now come for me to say good-bye, and really I cannot trust my feelings to say it as I should like to say it.

Believe me, I shall never forget you. In my sleep at night as well as in my waking hours, I shall hear in imagination the tramp of your feet in the yard, and see the lines of gray marching up and down.

And do not forget me. Think of me always as your true friend. I shall ask the privilege of being enrolled as an honorary member of your brotherhood.

I do not know that I could better close my remarks than by repeating to you those noble lines which the poet Longfellow found inscribed on a tablet in an old churchyard in the Austrian Tyrol:

"Look not mournfully into the Past; it comes not back again.

"Wisely improve the Present; it is thine.

"Go forth to meet the shadowy Future without fear and with a manly heart."

Halting and inadequate as are the words of my speech, I feel certain that my audience understands me. Had I stood up here and repeated the alphabet or the dictionary, I think it would have been the same. The men are going far behind the words; they are looking into my soul and I into theirs.

I have come among them, worn their uniform, marched in their lines, sat with them at meals and gone to the cells with them at night; for a week I have been literally one of them—even to fourteen hours in the dark punishment cells; what need therefore of words? It makes little or no difference what I say, or how far I fail to express my meaning. They understand.

A feeling of renewed life, a sense of hope and exhilaration kindles within me as I look in their faces and realize for the first time the full measure of their gratitude and affection. I step down from the platform and again take my seat with the basket-shop company; receiving warm grips of the hand from Stuhlmiller, Bell, and the others as I crowd past them to my seat in the center.

There ensues a long and dreary wait. In the mess-hall the first ones in are the first ones out; but up here in chapel the first ones in are the last ones out. It is a very tiresome arrangement for the earlier ones; and as we are well beyond the center, the delay seems interminable. Over thirteen hundred men have to march down stairs in single file, and that apparently takes a long time.

However, it gives a chance for my excitement to calm down, and my tired senses to get a bit rested. So that by the time I have marched down stairs, through the stone corridor, up the iron stairs and along the gallery to Cell 15, second tier, north, north wing, I am in a more normal condition than I have been since yesterday afternoon.

While I am packing my few belongings into the small

handbag, Grant appears at the door; and as soon as I am ready I accompany him for a last journey along the gallery, down the iron stairs and through the stone corridor. Then we turn up the stairway leading to the main office—the stairway down which I descended into prison six days ago. At the head of the flight two light taps on the iron door bring the face of the hall keeper to the pane of glass set in the door, the key grates in the lock and the heavy barrier swings open. I have passed the inner wall and breathe more freely.

Arrived in the Warden's rooms—he himself is unfortunately still away—I lose no time in getting into a tub. After a most refreshing bath, I dress in my ordinary citizen's clothes and am served with eggs and bacon and a cup of coffee. It is real coffee, not bootleg.

I do full justice to the food and drink, and feel very sorry for any one who has not had the experience of a first meal out of prison. I envy the Warden his cook and his devoted attendants.

After being thus invigorated, I gird up my loins for the next duty, and go to measure arguments with the Principal Keeper in his private office. I begin by shaking hands with him warmly, for I wish to atone for any rudeness of last night and make him understand that I have no hard feelings toward him personally. Then I plunge at once into the subject.

"P. K., I don't wish to be unpleasant, nor do or say anything I am not fully justified in doing or saying, but I must tell you plainly that I can not go from this place, leaving that poor sick boy down in that second cell in jail. There are others who, in my opinion, ought not to be there, but his is the worst case. He should be in the hospital, not in such a damnable hole as that. He's sick, and you are driving him crazy with your absurd rules about water. And I shall not—I can not—leave the prison unless something is to be done about it."

This and much more I pour into the patient ears of the P. K. It is written in the veracious "Bab Ballads," concerning Sir Macklin, a clergyman "severe in conduct and in conversation," that:

> "He argued high, he argued low,
> He also argued round about him."

It is much the same in this case. My arguments are many, and some are based on high moral ground and others on mere motives of self-interest. My words flow easily enough now.

The P. K. takes refuge behind the official policies. He disclaims any personal motives—almost any personal responsibility.

138

He seems to think that there is little or no occasion for the exercise of any judgment on his part. A complaint comes from an officer about a prisoner. There is apparently nothing for the P. K. to do but accept the complaint, take the word of the officer as a matter of course, and punish the prisoner. I also get the impression that sending every offender to the jail is the most desirable form of punishment, as it involves no troublesome discrimination or attempt at careful adjustment; it makes the thing so simple and easy.

Anything more crude, any greater outrage upon justice and common sense than the system of prison discipline as revealed in this illuminating discussion, it would be impossible to conceive. If a deliberate attempt were to be made to draft a code of punishment which should produce a minimum of efficacy and a maximum of failure and exasperation among the prisoners, it could not be more skilfully planned. One can no longer be surprised at the anomalous condition of things, as revealed by the kind of men I found in the jail.

In the midst of the discussion I welcome a warm ally in the Doctor, who at my request is brought into consultation. He had by no means intended that Number Two should be sent to the jail when discharged from the hospital; although he states it as a fact that the boy was a somewhat troublesome and unruly patient—a fact which I do not doubt in the least. Under existing conditions I should think any man, unless he were a dolt or an idiot, would be troublesome.

This statement of the Doctor's gives me the chance to utter a tirade against a System which has no gradation in its punishments. If stress is to be laid on punishment rather than reward, there should be at least some approximation to justice, and the punishment should bear some proportion to the offence. "You admit," I say to the P. K., "that these punishment cells are the severest form of discipline that you have. Then why, in Heaven's name, do you exhaust your severest punishment on trivial offences? If you use the jail with its dark cells and bread and water for whispering in the shop, what have you left when a man tries to murder his keeper?"

In reply the P. K. makes the best showing he can, but in truth there is no reply. One of the things that is most irritating about prison is the number of questions that admit of no sensible explanation. It irresistibly reminds one of the topsy-turvy world that Alice found in Wonderland; and of the Hatter's famous conundrum, "Why is a raven like a writing desk?" to which there was no answer.

The P. K., finding himself driven from point to point in the argument, takes refuge in the statement that complaint comes from the prison department in Albany that he doesn't punish often or severely enough. This seems very extraordinary. How in the world can the clerks in Albany judge of the need of punishments in this prison, concerning the inner workings of which they know absolutely nothing?

I argue, I implore, I threaten. The Doctor more gently and diplomatically seconds my efforts. Finally the P. K. with an air of triumph brings out his last and conclusive argument.

"There is a great deal in what you say, gentlemen, and I should like to oblige you, Mr. Osborne, but you see this is Sunday; and you know we never let 'em out of jail on Sunday."

The P. K. leans back in his chair, evidently feeling that he has used a clincher. Then I rise in wrath. "Sunday!" I exclaim. "In Heaven's name, P. K., what is Sunday? Isn't it the Lord's Day? Very well, then. Do you mean to tell us that you actually think if you take a poor sick boy, with an open wound in his ear, out of a close, dirty, vermin-filled, dark cell, where he isn't allowed to wash, and has but three gills of water a day—do you mean to say that to take that sick boy out of such a detestable hole and put him back into the hospital, where the Doctor says he belongs—do you really think that such an act of mercy would be displeasing to God? Do you think God approves of your infernal jail? Do you think——"

I break off, simply because I haven't the strength to continue; anger and disgust, on top of all the excitements of the last twenty-four hours, bring me to my last ounce of endurance. Fortunately the tide turns. The P. K. is silent for a few moments after my last outburst, but as I watch him I see something beginning to stir, a light is dawning upon the official mind, a smile of triumph announces a solution of the difficulty.

"Why," he gasps, "that's true. I think you're right. We put 'em in on Sunday; why shouldn't we take 'em out?"

The great question is solved. The P. K.'s brilliant logic has made it possible for mercy to temper justice, and pleased at his great discovery he determines to do the thing handsomely while he is about it, and let not only one but all the prisoners out of the jail. To this I have no objection to offer. He also generously accedes to my desire to pay a visit to these as yet unseen friends of mine; and I assure him that I will not pose as their deliverer, but simply give them good advice, and leave it for him to take them the news of their liberation.

On this errand I pass once more behind the barriers. I

140

descend the gloomy staircase from the rear office, and traverse part of my memorable walk of last night—through the stone corridor and down the yard to the jail office. Here the Captain in charge takes the heavy keys from the locker and opens the outer door. As our steps resound in the passage, I think how each of the five prisoners within is listening and wondering who and what is coming.

The inner door is unlocked and opened, and amid complete silence from the occupants of the other cells, Number Two's door is thrown open.

As I have said, it is a curious experience making acquaintance and establishing intimate relations with people whom you cannot see; but it is equally curious to see for the first time men with whose voices and personalities you already feel well acquainted. Last night I had the first of these experiences, now I have the other. One by one the cell doors are opened and the occupants, unwashed and in their dirty jail clothes, are allowed to step forward, shake me by the hand and have a few words of friendly conversation. I tell them I have come to see them face to face before leaving the prison, to thank them for their friendly treatment of me, to renew my invitation to dine when they leave, and to talk briefly over the case of each.

Number Two I advise to apologize to the Doctor. He admits being troublesome in the hospital; and it is quite evident the poor fellow needs to go back there. He is a dark-haired lad, with a sweet voice and a confiding, boyish manner that is very winning.

Number Three I advise to apologize to the Captain of his company and to try to keep his temper better in the future. The person who called him ugly names, having been sent to the hospital, seems to have been sufficiently punished. To my relief Number Three seems to be decidedly better of his cold.

Number Four (it is needless to say that my heart warms toward the handsome young fellow whom I greet as Joe) I advise to apologize to his Captain for the fight with Number Five, and to be more careful for the future. Joe is rather abashed and self-conscious by daylight, but very prolific of promises. Methinks he doth protest rather too much, and in spite of his good looks, his eyes do not give the direct glance that one likes to see.

To Number Five I give advice similar to Joe's, and he engages to profit by it.

To Number Eight I also urge an apology to the powers that be and submission to the inevitable. He is a little harder to convince than the others, but we reach an agreement.

"What is the use," I say to all of them, "of letting your tempers

141

get the better of you when it hurts nobody but yourselves?" My preaching is directed rather toward a cultivation of self-interest than of lofty idealism, but I believe it hits the mark. They none of them admit the justice of their jail sentences, and on that point I can not argue with them. I acknowledge the injustice, but ask them to face the facts. So one and all admit they have been wrong and express themselves ready to make all amends for the present and try their best for the future.

And so, in a much pleasanter frame of mind than when I last left this place, I retrace my steps to the Warden's rooms.

Returning through the back office I shake hands all around—with both officers and prisoners—all but one man. A slight, pale figure in glasses is bending over his desk in a corner of the office. He is one of the Warden's stenographers. Last July I had an extended conversation with him, at the Warden's suggestion, and a more hopeless and discouraging proposition I never struck. He is an old-timer, knows all the ropes, has been through the game, and has settled down to hopeless cynicism. He seems to have no belief in himself or others, and I have no doubt is utterly uninterested in my whole experience, and will be one of the greatest stumbling blocks to any attempted reforms. He will condemn them at the outset, discouraging others who are willing to try. This, at least, is the impression I had of him last July when the Warden persuaded me to talk with him. Now, as he bends over his desk with his eyes on his work I pass him by; for he evidently has no interest in me and I can not see where I can be of any service to him.

There remains now but one more thing to do—bid farewell to my partner, my dear and loyal friend, Jack Murphy. He has been sent for; and, as I reënter the Warden's office, he stands looking out of the window.

"Jack, old fellow, I couldn't leave here without saying good-bye to you."

He turns, and the tears are running down his cheeks. As for myself I have long since got beyond that stage. "Oh, Mr. Osborne——" he begins, but I stop him.

"Cut it out, partner, cut it out! You mustn't meddle with my last name. It has been Tom and Jack now since Wednesday, and Tom and Jack it must continue to be. I am still your partner, and clothes are not going to make any difference with you and me."

"Oh, Tom!" says the poor fellow. "What am I going to do now?"

For the first time I fully realize how deep this experience has

142

cut into the hearts of these men. I thought I already understood it, but Jack reveals a new depth.

"What are you going to do?" I ask in answer. "You are going right ahead making baskets down in the old shop. But you are also going to help out our Commission. While I am working outside, you will be working inside. And together, Jack, we are going to assist in giving things a good shaking up. You've got the hardest part of the work to do, but I shall keep in close touch with you, and we will often consult together. And sometime, Jack, some day in the future when the right time has come, you can count upon me to go to the Governor for you."

At this suggestion of a pardon, I expect to get from Jack a quick word of gratitude, some sort of indication that he is conscious of having attained his first step toward freedom, the interest of a friend who may be able to secure fair consideration, at least, of an application for pardon.

To my surprise he turns to me almost roughly. "Put that right out of your mind, Tom," he says. "Don't you bother your head about that, one single minute. I am ready to stay behind these walls all my life if I can help you and the Commission bring about some of these reforms you have in mind. That's all I want!"

I try to answer, but there is nothing to say. What can one do except to humble oneself before such a spirit of self-sacrifice? Moreover, while my whole being is thrilled with the wonder of all this new revelation of the essential nobility of mankind, my physical condition is approaching very near to complete collapse. Silently therefore I clasp Jack's hand in mine, and silently we stand looking out of the window while each of us masters his emotion. Then with a brief "Good-bye, Jack!" "Good-bye, Tom!" in the back office, I watch the heavy iron door close with a clang behind him, as he descends the iron staircase back into the prison; and so to his stone cage, four feet by seven and a half, in the damp basement of the north wing.

Then, with one last look through the grated window of the back office, I turn and make my way down the front steps of the prison. The guard at the gate unlocks and opens the outer barrier. I am free.

No, not free. Bound evermore by ties that can never be broken, to my brothers here within[Pg 279 the walls. My sentence, originally indeterminate, is now straight life, without commutation or parole.

It may be of interest, as a matter of record, to append a transcript of the official punishment report of the five prisoners with whom I spent the night in the jail.

143

Date	Reg. No.	Name	When Received	Location	Keeper	Punished by
Oct. 5	32648	N-L [16] [No. 3]	Dec. 30, 1912	Yard	H—[17]	A. P.K. [18]
	32812	E-D [No. 2]	Mar. 15, 1913	Yard	G—	"
	31175	A-J [No. 5]	July 18, 1910	State	M—	"
	31342	J-M [No. 4]	July 19, 1912	State	M—	"
	32465	J-W [No. 4]	Sept. 4, 1912	Enamel	F—	"

Pun. Cell Days	Days Forfeited	Compen-sation forfeited	Offense and Remarks.			
No. 3	3 days	10 days	$5.00 [19]	Striking another inmate while in yard.		
No. 2	3 days	10 days	$5.00	Disobeying orders by loud talking in hospital after being cautioned.		
No. 5	2 days	10 days	$5.00	Fighting with 31342. M—		
No. 4	2 days	10 days	$5.00	Fighting with 31175. J—		
No. 8	2 days	10 days	$5.00	Disobeying orders by refusing to work as told by officer and foreman.		

[16] The original has the full name.
[17] The original has the full name.
[18] A. P. K. = Acting Principal Keeper.
[19] Considerably more than a year's pay.

CHAPTER XV
CUI BONO?

February 1, 1914.

Since the eventful week I have attempted to describe in the foregoing chapters, I have received a large number of letters which throw light on the Prison Problem. Letters from the Auburn prisoners, letters from men in other prisons, letters from ex-convicts, giving ideas based upon their own experiences, letters from prison officials in other states, expressing keen interest in the results of my experiment, letters from sympathetic men and women of the outside world, proving the existence of a large amount of sentiment in favor of a rational reform of our Prison System.

Many of these letters are valuable in connection with the broad question of Prison Reform but have no direct bearing upon my personal experiences in Auburn Prison; they would therefore be out of place here. Others of them do deal directly with that incident, reflecting the prisoners' side of the matter. A selection from these letters has a distinct place in the story of my stay within the walls. If the tone of some of them seems unduly laudatory, let it be understood that they have been included not for that reason, but simply to enable us to gauge the actual results of the visit of Tom Brown—that fortunate representative of the sympathy of the outer world. These expressions of friendship and gratitude should not be considered as personal tributes, their importance lies not in the character of the recipient but in the state of mind of the writers.

In other words, the vital point of this matter, as in all others connected with the Prison Problem, is this: After all has been said and done, what manner of men are these prisoners? Are they specimens of "the criminal" we have had pictured to us in so many works on "Penology"? Or are they simply men from the same stock as the rest of us—some of them degenerate, some mentally ill balanced, some slaves to evil habits, diseased, sinful, or simply unfortunate—whatever you like—but still men? I think these letters may help others to an answer as they have helped me.

A few days after the memorable Sunday on which I left prison, Warden Rattigan found a paper placed upon his desk. It came from the slight, pale man with whom I had talked in July, the man who struck me as being such a cynic—so discouraged and discouraging, the one with whom I had not shaken hands upon leaving, because—

Heaven forgive me—I thought he had no interest or confidence in me or my experiment.

It seems, according to the Warden, that this man (his name is Richards) had at first been very sceptical concerning my visit; but he had, as will appear, watched me very carefully; and, after having changed his own point of view, was much irritated by certain sarcastic editorials in the newspapers. So he applied to the Warden for permission to write a letter on the subject to one of the great New York dailies.

When the Warden showed the letter to me I advised against its publication—as I cared for no personal vindication. But I treasured the letter, and Richards and I have since become the warmest of friends. Here is what he wrote to the Warden:

> I think that in justice to the prisoners in this institution that objection should be taken to some of the editorials which are being printed about Mr. Osborne's experience as a voluntary prisoner in Auburn prison. I for one desire to protest and take exception against some of the editorials which appear in the papers—especially in the New York A—— and S——.
>
> I have only used my privilege of letter writing on one occasion during my nearly two years' incarceration here, and I wish that I could be allowed to write to one of these papers a letter setting forth my exceptions in the following strain, and I want to assure you that I mean every word of what I have written.

The following is his draft of the proposed letter to the New York paper.

> I am one of those whom society calls a confirmed criminal. I have had the misfortune to be unable to resist temptation on several occasions, with the result that I carry upon my left sleeve the red disc of shame. But I want to say to you, and to the rest of the world, that although society looks upon me as a creature unworthy of sympathy, as one whose life has been a waste, as one not fit to associate with the people at large, yet I still have left within me a little spark of gratitude.
>
> I have watched with careful eye and keen interest this self-imposed imprisonment. My cell was very close to Tom Brown's, and at night I could look straight from my cell into

146

the window opposite and see there reflected the cell of Tom Brown, No. 15 on the second tier, and its occupant. I know that everything he went through was real. I know that there was no fake about his imprisonment. And I know this, that he went through a great deal more hardship and mental torture as a voluntary prisoner than he would had he been regularly committed to the prison. With his education and knowledge he would have been put to work in a clerical capacity, instead of making baskets, and his labor would not have been so hard. His incarceration in the cooler was real. I know this for a positive fact. I heard him coming from the cooler early Sunday morning in his stocking feet, so as not to wake up his fellow prisoners.

The editorial in the A— is unjust. It speaks of Jack London and others writing about prison conditions. It says that the convicts in the penitentiary "cannot get out," and that "they are locked in at night." Granted that all this is what you want to ridicule it to be, the man that wrote this editorial would be accused of being inhuman if he were to put his dog through what Mr. Osborne went through during his week of imprisonment.

There is one thing I want to emphasize, and it is this. Mr. Osborne has seen with his own eyes, heard with his own ears and felt with his own feelings just what it is to be an outcast, even for so short a time as a week—just what it is to be deprived of your liberty for even so short a period, and your editorial writers and no one else that has not gone through the actual experience are qualified to criticise his efforts.

These papers would not believe a prisoner who came out of prison and told you of these facts; you must believe Mr. Osborne—you can't do otherwise.

I want to say that this self-sacrifice is going to do much to make better men of us criminals, not only now but in the future when we are again thrust upon society; and if there was just a little more Osbornism and a little less Journalism the prisoners would have a greater incentive to reform than they now have.

I speak not only for myself, but for many other old timers with whom I have talked. I claim as an old timer and one who knows what he is talking about, as I have been through the mill since childhood, that one act of kindness will

147

do more toward reforming a criminal than a thousand acts of cruelty and than all the punishment that you can inflict.

Men will err, men will fall, and men will continue to commit crime, and society must be protected. We must have prisons; but I claim that the better way to treat a criminal in order to try and reform him is to use a little more kindness in our prisons and a little less punishment and cruelty.

I don't want to be misunderstood in this matter. I have no favor to ask of anyone. I expect to do my time—all of it. But I want to take exception to the insinuation that Mr. Osborne's stay was made any softer by the fact that the editor of his paper is Warden of Auburn Prison. The fact is that Warden Rattigan was away from the prison during the most of the week of Mr. Osborne's imprisonment, and I know positively and from my own knowledge that his orders were to treat Tom Brown the same as any other convict in this prison; and 1,329 men here can testify that these orders were carried out to the letter.

If some of these editorial writers could have heard the spontaneous applause in our chapel when Mr. Osborne, clad in the garb of a convict, rose from his seat and walked to the platform to address us, and could have seen the tears in the eyes of hardened rogues, I am sure that they would never treat this experiment in the light way they do. It was really a sorrowful and heart-rending spectacle and one which will never be forgotten by those who witnessed it. And if they could have witnessed the tears which flowed from Mr. Osborne's eyes after he had once again put on the clothes of civilization, they would have been convinced that his heart was almost breaking for the men whom he was leaving for a time.

I am firmly convinced that Mr. Osborne is as much a friend of society as he is of the prisoner—there is no question about that; that he has at heart the interest and welfare of society, as well as the interests of the under dog, and that his motives are not inspired by any wholly sympathetic feeling, but by a feeling of brotherly love and justice and the feelings of one who believes in all of the words in the little line of the Lord's Prayer:

"Forgive us our trespasses, as we forgive those who trespass against us."

L. Richards, No. 31—.

I leave it for any one to judge whether the writer of that letter is a hopeless criminal. Yet he speaks of himself as an old-timer, who bears upon his sleeve that cruel symbol of a repeated failure to make good—"the red disc of shame."

To gauge this one man's ability, his latent power for good, I add another letter from him, written at a time when the whole prison population was fearful that the new order of things in the prison department of New York State might be upset by the change of governors.

> Auburn Prison,
>   October 20, 1913.
> Mr. Thomas Mott Osborne, Auburn, N. Y.
> My dear Sir:
> I learn of your expected visit to Albany during the present week, and I most earnestly request that if you take up any of the matters with reference to the work of your Commission, that you present a plea of the prisoners here for a continuance of the work which you have started.
> I have read numerous criticisms of your acts, most of them coming to the one conclusion—that you could not during your stay here undergo mentally what other prisoners were enduring. I know that was not calculated on by you; and I, as well as quite a number of others with whom I have spoken, fully understand and appreciate your motive.
> Were not one of your ideas adopted, were not a single thing done to better the physical condition of the prisoners in the penal institutions of the state, yet you have brought into our hearts and minds a desire to make better men of ourselves, to prove to the world that kindness and not punishment is the reformative agency.
> We wonder what there is in us that impels men to take up our cause. I have given considerable thought to this in my solitary moments at night, and have come to the conclusion that there must be some good still left in even the most wretched and degenerate, that there must be some seed of righteousness, some spirit of manhood still left which only needs the proper nourishment to bring it into life. Punishment has been tried for centuries, and has failed. The doctrine of kindness and brotherly feeling as set forth by you will, I am sure, succeed; and I wish that you would plead our cause and lay before the proper authorities the importance of continuing the work.

A spirit of hope has sprung up in our hearts. Is this to be crushed and turned to despair? Are we to see the efforts of your Commission defeated at this time? God forbid.

I do not plead for myself. I plead for the wives and the innocent babes of some of our unfortunates. For their sakes, if for no other reason, this work should continue. I know that the prisoners here will show by their conduct, not only now but in the future, that they have been influenced to do good and to do right, by the efforts which you have made and are making in their behalf.

I am one of those dyed deep with crime, in the opinion of society. I have been in several prisons, but I still feel that I have a chance, that there is still hope; and this feeling has been strengthened within the past month by your act of self-sacrifice; and I see around me 1,300 other men whose lives are worth something to society—worth the effort which your Commission is making for their uplift.

Very truly yours,

L. Richards, No. 31—.

It may be urged that Richards is a man of very considerable literary ability, which is obvious, and that his case is an exceptional one.

Let us, therefore, take a man of entirely different caliber, of but little education, one whose experience has been a rough one. Following is a letter from a man who is as unlike Richards mentally and physically as one man can very well be from another.

135 State St., Auburn, N. Y.

Oct. 5, 1913.

Mr. Thomas M. Osborne.

Honorable Sir: It affords me great pleasure to write you these few lines. I really do not know how to begin to express myself as I have not got a very good education. But I hope you will understand that my motive in writing you this letter is to congratulate you for your good work. I fully realize the fact that it was no easy task for you to come down here and live here in this place for one week as you did. After hearing and seeing you in the chapel Sunday I came to my cell and got to thinking. The outcome was that I could not remember ever being touched so as I was when I left the chapel and while sitting there hearing you talk. I fully realize what a big thing you have undertaken. At one time I was

150

under the impression that there was no such a thing as a square man, but I have changed my opinion and I am safe in saying that quite a number of other men have also changed their mind about that same thing.

***

Men who love their fellow man are very few. When I think of you I am reminded of a postal that I received from my brother not long ago, after him not knowing that I was in prison. When he found it out he sent me a postal and on it were these few words: "A friend is one who knows all about you and likes you just the same." Well, Mr. Osborne, I leave here on the 20th of this month and believe me—never again for me. I have played the crooked game in every way it can be played, most every kind of crooked game there is. Now I am done. It is a fast and excitable game, but I come to realize that it is not living and is bound to come to a bad end. But I want to say that prison life did not reform me, nor will it reform any man, for no man learns good in prison. My opinion is that the only way that a man can be reformed is get to his conscience, wake up the man in him. You are aware of the fact that the police make many criminals. I don't believe there is such a thing as a hardened criminal. If the police were not so anxious to send men to prison there would be no so-called hardened criminals. I know what I am talking about. There are too many men sent to prison innocently and there will always be so-called hardened criminals until that is stopped. I done my first bit innocently. Believe me, it is a terrible thing to sit in one of those cells and know in your heart that you are there in the wrong. Well I wish I had the paper to write you more for I deem it a pleasure to write you.

Yours truly,
James McCabe, No. 32.—

Soon after receiving this letter and before his release, I had an interview with the writer. I found him a very frank and engaging person, a crook by profession, with most excellent ideas on the subject of Prison Reform—which was the main topic of our conversation.

On the day of his release Jim visited me at my office; my first thought was that he had come to strike me for money, but I did him

151

injustice. He came simply to ask my interest and help for a young man who locked in on his gallery and in whom he had become interested.

"Can't you do something for him, Tom," he urged. "That kid's no crook. If you can only keep him out of the city he'll go straight. He sure will. You see him and have a talk with him, and see if you don't think so."

That was all Jim wanted of me, and at first he refused to take the small loan I pressed upon him, although the money he received from the state would not go very far in New York City. "I don't want to take it, Tom," he objected, "and I'll tell you why. You'd be giving me that money thinking I was going straight. Now I'm going to try to go straight; but you've no idea of the difficulties. How am I going to get an honest job? The cops all know me well, they'll follow me wherever I go. I can't enter a theater, I can't get on to a street car. If anything happens I'll be one of the first men the coppers'll be after. How much of a chance have I to get an honest job? Now, if I take your money and then didn't go straight I should feel like the devil."

"Jim," said I, "you'll take that money because you are going straight. I'll bank on you."

My confidence was not misplaced. Jim went to New York and, having the luck to have a home with a good mother and a brother who is straight, Jim had time to hunt his job until he found it. About two weeks after his release Jim lunched with me in New York, and in the course of conversation remarked, "Say, Tom, don't you think there's such a thing as an honest crook?"

"Sure, Jim," I answered, "you're one."

A little taken aback by this direct application, Jim said, "Well, you know what I mean. I'll tell you a case. There was three of us pulled off a little piece of business once, and afterward one of those fellows wanted me to join with him and freeze out the other fellow. Now, that's what I don't call honest, do you?"

"I certainly do not," I said. "And now I'll tell you what was in my mind. I call you an honest crook, Jim, because while you've been a crook you have been square with your pals. Because the operations of your mind are honest, you haven't tried to fool yourself. There is nothing the matter with your mental operations. You have been simply traveling in the wrong direction. Make up your mind to shift your course, and you'll have no trouble going straight, because you are naturally an honest man."

Space forbids my going further into Jim's interesting history, but up to the time of writing my diagnosis seems to have been

152

correct. Jim has a good job, is going straight, and just before Christmas he said to me, "Tom, I never was so happy in my life!"

How many more men like Jim are there in prison? Are they not worth saving?

Jim said in his letter, "Prison life did not reform me, nor will it reform any man." That is true; and no man will find help in prison for reforming himself until the conditions are greatly changed—until a system has been established in which a man can gain some sense of civic responsibility toward the community in which he lives. If such a sense of responsibility could be developed while in prison, would it not greatly help in a man's conduct after his release?

The following is not a letter, but a typewritten statement which Grant, the Superintendent of Prison Industries, found on his desk the morning after my last day's talk in chapel. One of the prisoners in Grant's office, upon returning to his cell, had felt moved to write down a description of the incident. This is it.

Sunday, Oct. 5, 1913.

Truly the past week, and to-day in particular, will mark an epoch in the history of Auburn Prison, if indeed, it does not in the entire state.

Mr. Osborne's stay among us has awakened new thoughts and higher ideals among the men confined here than any other agency hitherto tried or thought of.

His coming as he did, precisely the same as the most lowly of malefactors, and receiving no better treatment than would be accorded any others, has awakened feelings among the majority that can hardly be credited, much less described.

Those who in the past week have written articles in the various newspapers ridiculing Mr. Osborne's experiment, would have been put to shame had they been present at the chapel services this morning.

Never in my life before have I witnessed such a scene. When the Chaplain invited Thomas Brown to the platform, the audience could hardly restrain themselves, so great was their enthusiasm. It was at least five minutes before Mr. Osborne could be heard, and during his remarks it was about all any of us could do to keep the tears back.

As he ascended the platform, garbed as the rest of the audience, minus his usual attire but with the same air of determination and force that has always characterized him, he was greeted by the Chaplain and some ladies and gentlemen from one of the churches here; and his acknowledgment of the greeting was exactly as courteous and dignified as if he had not just been through one of the most memorable experiences of his life; and one could not help seeing the man and not the clothes he wore.

His remarks were of a character to cheer the downhearted and to urge to stronger endeavor for the right those who have made errors and find the path none too easy. His advice, as usual, was listened to with the greatest attention, and I have never seen an audience so wholly and unreservedly with a speaker as the boys seemed to be with him.

Where can you find a man who has the many interests that Mr. Osborne has, who will give up everything he has been accustomed to, and risk his health, yes, you might almost say his life—for one never knows what may occur in an institution of this kind—for the sake of those who are apparently nothing to him? We might understand it better if he were doing this for some immediate member of his family, instead of for strangers and outcasts.

***

Of one thing we are sure, and that is that Thomas Mott Osborne will never be forgotten by the inmates of this prison, and I firmly believe that he has been the means of inspiring love for himself in the hearts of the men here that will never die. In my own case, at least, I can speak with certainty. Although I have never spoken to the man in my life and never expect to, he has certainly inspired thoughts in my heart that never were there before; or if they were, they have been so warped and obstructed by the exigencies of my life for ten years past that I did not realize that I possessed them at all.

He is a man who is entitled to the best love of every human being that comes within the range of his influence, whether they know him personally or not. And he has won hearts to-day that nobody else on earth could.

In closing let me repeat his last words to us this morning. I shall always remember them.

"Look not mournfully upon the past; it cannot return.

"The present is yours; improve it.

"Fear not the shadowy future; approach it with a manly heart."

154

This is as I recall it. It may possibly not be exact—
however the sense is the same.

If Mr. Osborne half realized what an influence for good
his stay here had been to every single man in the place, I feel
sure that he would not feel that his privations and hardships
of the past week had been in vain.

Sincerely,

E. O. I., No. 32—.

Of course it may be urged with some force that such letters are
not conclusive, for it can not be proved that the writers have
received any permanent help; that even those, like Jim, who
straighten out may get tired of a virtuous life and relapse. That is
perfectly true. For instance, my lively jail friend in Cell Four, Joe, in
spite of all efforts to help him upon his release, failed to make good.

But such an argument misses the point. The important thing
is that these men have good in them—a statement that can not be
made too often. It is true that they are bad—in spots. But they are
also good—in spots. And with a right system the good could be
developed so as to help in driving out the bad. If Joe had received
proper training in prison he would have gone straight after he got
out. What I am just now trying to prove is the existence of good—
and a large measure of it.

Here, for instance, is a letter from a man who has failed to go
straight since his release.

135 State St., Auburn, N. Y.,

Sunday, Oct. 19, 1913.

Hon. Thomas Mott Osborne, Auburn, N. Y.

Dear Sir: As this is the last letter yours truly will ever
write in a prison cell (that is, I hope to God and his blessed
and holy Mother it is the last), I don't know of a person other
than T. M. Osborne I would rather write to. I don't know of a
single case ever recorded in the U. S. if not in the world
where fourteen hundred men left a meeting house—men,
understand, in public life who would not stop at anything—
those same men left that chapel on Oct. 5 crying like babies!
And I, being prison steam-fitter here, I heard some very
good stories of Mr. Osborne—going around to the different
shops Monday morning. It only shows that with a little
kindness shown toward these same men that you could do
most anything with them, and make better men of them in
the future. Before God, I honestly swear and believe that Mr.

155

Osborne could have taken that same bunch of men from Auburn Prison that Sunday, and put them on the road to work and 99 per cent. would have made good—and that's a very good percentage. I have seen a good deal of this country—east, west, north and south—but believe me Oct. 5 beats everything. It is a scene which I shall always remember. Well, Mr. Osborne, I expected to have a little talk with you on Prison Reform but you have been very busy, so if I get a chance some time I'll drop in and see you. I leave the Hotel Rattigan to-morrow morning a wiser and better man.

Believe me, sir, you have the love and respect of every man behind these prison walls.

With God's blessing, a long life and a happy one to you, dear sir.

I beg to remain yours truly,

Tom Curran, Steamfitter, Auburn Prison.

I am going to work Tuesday morning at my trade in Syracuse.

The writer, Curran is not his real name, also refused to accept a loan of money which I offered to him so that he could fit himself out with the tools of his trade. He did not get the job in Syracuse, but drifted into another state to a city where, quite by chance three months later, I ran across him in the county jail. The trouble with Tom was the same as in the case of so many others. Perfectly straight when sober, he could not help stealing when drunk, and he hadn't enough strength of mind to keep out of saloons. How could he have? What had the prison done to aid him in developing strength of character?

The following letter is a very characteristic one.

Auburn, N. Y., October 6, 1913.

Mr. Thomas M. Osborne.

Dear Sir: I trust you will pardon the liberty I take in writing you. But I wish to thank you for the interest you have taken in the men here. I know there are hundreds of people who have our interests at heart, but they imagine we are a sort of strange animal, and treat us as such. You know if you put a dog in a cage for five or ten years, he will become unfit as a pet. Just so with us, we enter here intending to become better men, but the treatment we receive from some of those

156

who are in immediate charge of us, causes us to become embittered at the world in general.

You have done more good in the past few days than any other man or woman interested in Prison Reform. You was not ashamed to make yourself one of us (if only for a week); you lived as we live, ate what we ate, and felt the iron hand of discipline. You came among us as man to man and I heartily thank you for it. When you stood in the chapel last Sunday, and talked to us like a father with tears in your eyes and hardly able to speak, I prayed as I never prayed before, and asked God to care for you and watch over you in your coming struggle to better conditions here. I know you will meet with opposition both here and outside. By that I do not mean the Warden, as he has proven himself to be a just man in every respect. I mean those who are in immediate charge of us. Some of them are not in accord with your project, and showed their disapproval by reprimanding us for greeting you as we did last Sunday. But they are not to blame in one sense, for they have been here so long their feelings have become stagnated and any new movement appears to them an intruder. They may be in a position to prevent us from showing our feelings physically, but, thank God, they cannot control us mentally. And just so long as I can think, so long will I think of you as our friend.

You have caused the men here to see things in a different light, and you can be assured of their utmost loyalty; for I do not believe there is a man here who would not call you his friend. And in closing I wish to thank Warden Rattigan and Supt. Riley for their hearty support of you, and hope to God I may be able some day to thank you in person. I am now and always,

Loyally yours,
Frank Miller, No. 32—, Auburn Prison.

Certain fundamental facts have never been more clearly expressed than in the first paragraph of that letter. People "imagine we are a sort of strange animal, and treat us as such." The prisoners "enter here intending to become better men," but the treatment they receive "causes us to become embittered at the world in general."

There is the Prison Question in a nutshell.

Perhaps it will be remembered that each evening at 6:40, while in my cell, I heard a violin played with rare feeling. Two weeks after my visit ended I made the acquaintance of the player—a young man who received me with rather painful embarrassment. He had an air of constraint and reticence as I spoke of his probable intention to make use of his talent after leaving prison. He told me that he was a graduate of Elmira, and also of the United States navy. I left him with the feeling that our interview had not been very much of a success. I was therefore the more surprised to receive the following letter a few days afterward.

135 State St., Auburn, N. Y.,
Oct. 17, 1913.
Hon. Thos. M. Osborne, Auburn, N. Y.
Dear Sir: Ever since Tuesday I have been trying to muster up sufficient courage to write you. After you left and I had finally regained control of myself it occurred to me that I had forgotten to ask you inside; but coming as you did I was completely taken by surprise and forgot everything, for which I hope you will pardon me.

Your unexpected visit, brief as it was, furnished me much food for thought. I can not truthfully say that I was not flattered by your kind approbation—but it has not turned my head; to the contrary, it has caused me to think a bit harder than I ever have before. As you undoubtedly know by your brief experience here, the subject which occupies a man's mind mostly is reflection; and while a large amount of my time has been tempered with reflection, up until now it had never led me into this particular channel.

I have made various plans as to the course I shall pursue in regaining all that I have lost, when I shall have been released. But until now I had never considered music as the medium to accomplishing this end. Perhaps I am overestimating my ability—I probably am—but at least I mean to attempt it. When I was sentenced to Elmira I cursed the day that I ever learned to play; after I had been there a while I began to miss my violin even more than the cigarettes of which I was likewise deprived. As the time progressed, and I was not getting any nearer home, through non-compliance with the rules, I finally banished music from my mind and everything connected with it; and from then on I seemed to get on better.

The period I was in the navy was too strenuous to admit of anything but adapting myself to the life; with the exception of dodging ex-convicts with which the navy is amply supplied.

After I found myself beached and began life again, I had completely forgotten the fact that I had ever played unless some one who knew me of old questioned me in this regard.

It was not until I came here that I had the desire to play at all, and never while here has that desire framed into a resolve until now. Were I never to see you again I will always remember you, your kindness has awakened long buried impulses.

I have gone into this thing further than I intended; my intention was to thank you for your kindness in coming to see me. I little thought when you came into the P. K.'s office to have your record taken, the first day of your self-imposed term, that I should be in your thoughts even for a little while. I knew you were over me when I commenced to play, but never dreamed or hoped that it would have any more than a passing effect upon you. And when I passed you at different times I avoided you, as I did not think there was anything about me which would attract your interest, knowing as I do how little consideration I deserve from anyone.

Your kindness will never be forgotten. Nothing can happen during the remainder of my term which will afford me greater happiness. A happiness accompanied with a deep regret for all that I have neglected and opportunities unaccepted, but for which I thank you from the bottom of my heart.

Very respectfully,
Charles F. Abbott (P. K.'s Clerk),
Auburn Prison, October 17, 1913.

I think most schools and colleges might be successfully challenged to show a letter better expressed or showing a finer spirit of manliness. In fact one finds in all these letters, and in many others not included here, a peculiar note of clearness; it is to be found also in the talk of many of these men, after you have succeeded in gaining their confidence; a rare note of sincerity and strength—as if the unimportant hypocrisies of life had been burned away in their bitter experiences.

In the month of December, 1913, immediately upon my return from a six weeks' business trip to Europe, I visited my friends at the prison. Then I found that my shopmate, Jack Bell, had been transferred to Clinton Prison on account of his health. A day or two

159

later I received the following acknowledgment of some postcards I had sent him.

Dannemora, New York, Sunday, Dec. 14, 1913.
The Hon. Thomas Mott Osborne.

Dear friend: A line to try and explain to you the way I am longing to again have the pleasure of seeing and speaking to you. After I received your cards, which were very pretty, it is only necessary for me to say here that I appreciated your loving kindness of thinking to send them. By this time no doubt you know of my transfer from Auburn to Dannemora which I thought would not be. But now that it has, I am pleased to say all is well, and find this place better than my previous home; see! There is only one thing I regret, and that is I'll not have as many opportunities of seeing and talking with you. For in the short time spent in your company can only say I miss your presence more and more. If in the future you will write me a line or so, such will cheer me in my moments of thought. Would be pleased to hear of your trip abroad. I hope you had a more pleasanter time than while at Auburn. I can not say in this letter the way I appreciated your cards. I sat for some time looking at them and thinking. I must say in closing that you have my sincere wishes for a merry Christmas, as this is the last letter till after it has passed. May you enjoy it and many to come. Give Jack my love and tell him to be good.
Believe me to be sincerely yours,
John J. Bell.

Once I heard Bell described as "just an ordinary fellow who likes to appear tough." Reading between the lines of his letter I think one can discern the fine instincts of a gentleman. I thought I recognized such when I met him in the basket-shop; this letter and others I have had from him confirm that belief.

As I think my narrative must have shown, there is a very soft spot in my heart for my comrades of the dark cells. It has been a source of deep regret to me that Joe, Number Four, did not make good on his release; and I hope that the others will have stronger purposes and better results.

Perhaps there may be some interest in the fate of the poor lad in Cell Two, who tipped over his water, and whose mental and physical sufferings added so much to my own distress during that horrible night. Upon his release the next day he went back to the hospital, where he remained for some time. In the month of November, while I was in Europe, he wrote me the following letter.

135 State St., Auburn, N. Y.,
Monday, Nov. 16, 1913.
My dear Friend, "Number One":

How little those words convey, and again how much. That I may write them to you, in the consciousness that they mean all that the words "dear friend" imply, is a greater happiness than I dared hope for. I have been in "Lunnon" with you for the past two weeks. That means, I have been allowing myself the daily luxury of thinking of you, and now the rare one of writing.

I presume you are wondering if I have been to the bungaloo since your departure. No, sir! My promise will hold good. In the past I have formed good resolutions, not one but many. Most of them died in their infancy; others lived long enough to make me unhappy. This time, though, circumstances are different, and I sincerely hope that confidence placed in me will not have been wasted.

Number One, did you ever have the blues—real, dark, deep indigo, bluey blues? I do frequently, and the cause I attribute to my ear. There is a continual buzzing, with short, shooting pains; and the doctors have informed me there is no cure. I receive a syringe of twenty-five per cent. alcohol daily, that gives relief for the time being. Well, Thanksgiving is near at hand; so I ought to be thankful that my other ear is not performing like a motor in need of oil. Believe me, I am.

Mr. Peacock called Sunday (8th) and we had an agreeable talk. He seemed a very pleasant gentleman, and warned me to walk a chalk line, so you see I dare not go to jail. As you once upon a time were in prison, to a certain extent, you realize what pleasures a visit brings. I appreciate yours, Mr. P.'s, and Mr. Rattigan's kindness very much.

***

I know all the boys would wish to be remembered if they knew I were writing. I didn't tell them for that would mean fifty sheets of paper, and I hadn't the nerve to ask Mr. R. for that. But I will say this: that we all want to hear, see, and talk to our own Tom Brown, even if he is an ex-convict. Don't let our English cousins keep you over there too long.

161

Wishing you the best of everything, I am, anxiously awaiting a letter, your Jail Friend Number Two—or Edward R. Davis, No. 32—.

Is it merely prejudice that makes me think that letter an exceptionally charming one? Has that boy no good in him worth developing?

These letters are enough, I believe, to prove my point. I could give many more, including those from Dickinson who, united with his wife and children, is working honestly and happily at his trade, earning money to pay his obligations and justifying the Chaplain's faith in his character. But there is not space for all the letters, so I have selected only those which seem to show most clearly what they all show—the good that is in the hearts of all men, even those who have seemed to be most evil; the wonderful possibilities which lie stored up, five tiers high, in our prisons.

Room must be made, however, for one short missive which I found on my desk the Sunday I came out of prison. It was anonymous and came from New York City. It reads as follows.

Damn Fool! Pity you are not in for twenty years.

The postmark is that of the substation in the city which is nearest to a certain political headquarters on Fourteenth Street.

Is there any possible connection between these two facts? Perish the thought!

One more before closing this bundle of letters. In the first chapter reference was made to a friend to whom I first mentioned my plan of going to prison. Soon after that incident I received a letter from him enclosing one coming from an imaginary Bill Jones to the imaginary Tom Brown. Its cleverness, its wisdom, its underlying pathos, its witty characterization of social conditions and their relation to the Prison Problem make it a real contribution to the discussion.

Oct. 9, 1913.
Hon. T. M. Osborne, Auburn, N. Y.
My dear Friend: Enclosed you will please find a note for a very dear friend of mine, Tom Brown by name, who was recently released from Auburn Prison. Brown is a perfectly good fellow, although you wouldn't believe so if you were to judge him by his prison record alone; but the truth of the matter is that he is a party of decided views, possessing an

individuality of his own; and being of this type he was bound to bump into things while on the inside looking out.

Hand him this note, do what you can for him, and believe me as ever,

Yours most sincerely,

W—— N. R——.

Enclosed in this letter was the following.

Oct. 9, 1913.
Thomas Brown, Esq.,
Auburn, N. Y.
Dear Tom:

I note by the papers that you have served your bit and are now out again digging around for your own meal ticket.

I also note from the same informative sources, that following your usual proclivity for action, you started something while in the hash foundry, and consequently got a fine run for your money; the result being that you were shook down for your large and munificent earnings when discharged, and turned loose on a warmhearted world without any change in your jeans. But why worry? You've got a good and lucrative trade now, learned at the expense of the state of New York; and you know as well as I do that a good clever basket and broom maker, besides becoming a competitor of the unhappy blind, who are wont to follow this trade, can also earn as much as one dollar per day weaving waste-paper baskets for the masses.

I also note that a guy by the name of Osborne interviewed you after your release, and that you immediately put up a howl about your not liking the basic principles which call such joints as the one which you just quitted into existence; and that as per usual the foresighted and profound-thinking editorial writers on several of the big New York joy-sheets, which are published as accessories to the Sunday comic supplements, immediately broke into song and wanted to know what in hell you expected such places to be.

But don't mind these newspaper stiffs, Tom. One discovers on coming in personal contact with them that, as a rule, their writings are all based on inexperience and the writers may be classified as belonging to the same species as Balaam's ass. So forget them.

I know this Osborne party personally; and take it from me that if he had been born and brought up in the neighborhood of the gas-house he'd sure have been some rough-neck. He is full of pep and actually thinks for himself. He also has some peculiar ideas relative to the rights and duties of humanity, and your experiences truthfully related to him will probably bring results.

This Osborne guy is no novice in prison dope, and for years has been beefing about society throwing away its so-called "waste material," when it might just as well be turned into valuable by-products by an intelligent application of the laws of synthetic social chemistry.

It's his dope that if some Dutch guy can beat it into some big industrial joint, say like those of the United States Steel Company or the Standard Oil, and by an intelligent application of the laws of nature change waste material into valuable by-products and big dividends, that it is up to society to experiment a little with its social junk pile and see what a little of the right kind of chemistry will do to the waste material to be found therein.

I can distinctly remember when the big blast furnaces around this man's town were cussed right along for dumping slag and cinders into the local river as waste material. The aborigines and other natives hereabouts used to form committees to call on our old college friend, Andy Carnegie, and tell him about it. Andy, of course, felt badly, but used to come back with a "What's biting you people, anyway? Nobody can eat this slag, can they?" He had to put his waste somewhere, so why not use the rivers? Along about this time, however, in blows a Dutch boy named Schwab, he studies the question of slag and other waste material and its utilization; and now said slag is converted into high grade cement, price, $15 per ton, f. o. b. cars, Pittsburgh, Pa.

Ditto the juice from the oil refineries which polluted the rivers when I was a kid. At present writing this former waste material that used to wring hectic curses from all the river water-users from Pittsburgh to Cairo is changed into thirty-two separate compounds; and yet some people actually think that John D. stole his coin when the truth of the matter is that he simply hired a guy to study out plans for the utilization of waste and then beat the other stiffs to it before they were next.

Same way with the slaughter houses. When Charley

164

Murphy was wiping his beezer on the bar towel and asking, "Wot'll youse guys have next?" most every town had an unlovely spot known as the slaughter-house district, and property was valued in an increasing ratio based on its distance therefrom. Because why? Foul-smelling waste. But along comes P. Armour, Esq., studies the waste question and says to the slaughter-house stiffs, "Gimme the leavings and other things you throw away and I'll not only put Chicago on the map, but I'll likewise build one of the loveliest trusts that ever allowed a fourth-rate lawyer to bust into public life by the attacking of the same."

Well, that's what's wrong with this Osborne party. While he lets other ginks browse around the waste-heaps of the mills and factories seeing what can be done with their junk, he pokes around in the social waste-heap trying to find out if its contents can't be converted into something useful. One might call him a social engineer; though as a rule men of original and new ideas are usually called nuts. But be that as it may, I note that Stevenson, Bell, Morse, Edison, and a whole list of folks who have done useful things, were at one time classed as being a bit odd but harmless.

As there are no personal dividends in the way of kale coming to any one who tries to convert the social waste-heap into something useful, the average stiff can't understand why a guy with a bean on him like Osborne should want to waste his good time monkeying with it, when he might be more socially useful by inventing a new tango step.

You see, Tom, society is so constituted at present that it can't understand why any man should want to do something that will bring him no financial returns; and yet this self-same society, that does all of its reasoning on a dollar and cents basis, can't understand why some poor stiff interred in a penal institution should register a kick against being compelled to work five, ten, or fifteen years for nothing.

Society also doesn't seem to realize that it constitutes and creates its own temptation—to wit, when a gink sizes up the class of stiffs big cities like New York and elsewhere pick up to run their public business, and the shake-downs they stand for from their own duly chosen and elected grafters, the little gink feels it to be his almost bounden duty to stock up a flossy silver quarry and lead them to it.

Of course there have been many changes in prison conditions since this Osborne party got fussing around, both inside and out, but nevertheless there is still room for more. Speaking of old conditions, I am personally acquainted with a party who could throw a piece of Irish confetti up in the air, and who, if he didn't duck, would get it on his conk and be reminded of old times, who can most distinctly remember when the social unit who happened to land in the waste heap lost his hair, manhood, and faith in man and God Almighty, all inside of twenty-four hours.

This was in the days of zebra clothing, short hair, the lock-step, contract labor, and all around soul-murder.

I know, however, that there have been many changes since then; so that although your experience, while proving that the great and assinine waste of good material is still going on in the social mill, and therefore most heart-stirring, will never carry with it the soul-blighting memories of one who for fourteen years marched the lock-step.

Of course, now that you are free, you will be in for your knocks as an ex-con and all that, but why worry? You will still have the privilege of the free air with opportunity always before you. Of course you are bound to meet with that duty loving stiff who knowing of your having been in the social waste heap believes in advertising the fact. But again, why worry? If you feel that you can make good—why?

Some time I want to tell you about my old friend O'Hoolihan and the bird. He spent twenty-seven years in the place you just left and made one of the greatest sacrifices for a little robin redbreast that I ever knew a man to make—well, say for the benefit of a bird.

Yours very truly,
Bill Jones.

166

CHAPTER THE LAST
THE BEGINNING

February 15, 1914.
"The vilest deeds, like poison weeds,
Bloom well in prison air;
It is only what is good in Man
That wastes and withers there."

So wrote the poet of Reading Gaol, whose bitter expiation has left an enduring mark in literature. But the lines do not express the whole truth. The Prison System does its best to crush all that is strong and good, but you can not always destroy "that capability and god-like reason" in man. Out of the prison which man has made for his fellow-man, this human cesspool and breeding place of physical, mental and moral disease, emerge a few noble souls, reborn and purified.

All about me while I was in prison—that hard and brutal place of revenge, I felt the quiet strivings of mighty, purifying forces—the divine in man struggling for expression and development. Give these forces free play, and who knows what the result may be? The spirit of God can do wondrous things when not thwarted by the impious hand of man.

It will not be forgotten, I hope, the conversation Jack Murphy and I had about the formation of a Good Conduct League among the prisoners. My partner lost no time in getting the affair under way. On the very afternoon of our parting in the Warden's office he wrote me the following letter. It is made public with considerable reluctance, because it seems like violating a sacred confidence. On the other hand when I spoke to Jack about the matter his reply was characteristic. "Print it if you want to, Tom. Whatever I have said or written you can do anything you like with; and especially if you think it will help the League."

So here is the letter.

Sunday, Oct. 5, 1913.
My dear friend Tom:
No doubt you must think me a great big baby for the way I acted while in your presence this afternoon. I had no idea that you would call upon me so soon after your release, although I hardly think it would of made any difference

whether it had of been a week from this afternoon; I would have acted the same.

The week that I spent working by your side was the most pleasant as well as the most profitable one of my life, and God, how I hated to see you go.

But your lecture this A. M. in chapel was the most wonderful I ever heard. Many was the heart that cried out its thankfulness to God for sending you into us, and many a silent promise was made to the cause for which you gave up a week of your happiness and freedom to solve.

And Tom, you have made a new man of me, and all that I ask and crave for is the chance to assist you in your works. I would willingly remain behind these "sombrous walls" for the rest of my life for this chance. I know and feel that I can do good here, for there are a good many in here that knows me by reputation; and if I could only get them under my thumb and show them that it does not pay to be a gangist or a crook, or a tough in or out of prison. As I told you to-day, I have no self-motive for asking this request; for if successful I know and feel that the reward which awaits you in the hereafter mayhap awaits me also; and I am willing to sacrifice my freedom and my all in order to gain the opportunity of once more meeting face to face and embracing my good, dear mother whom I know is now in Heaven awaiting and praying for me.

To-morrow, Monday, Oct. 6, I shall request one of the boys in the basket-shop to draw up a resolution pledging our loyalty to your cause; and I shall ask only those who are sincere to sign it. After this has been done I am going to ask our Warden for permission to start a Tom Brown League; its members to be men who have never been punished. Tom, I hope that you and your fellow-commissioners as well as Supt. Riley and Warden Rattigan will approve of this, for I am sure that such a League will bring forth good results. I have associated so many years among the class of men in this prison that I believe them to be part of my very being; and that is why I have so much confidence in the success of a Tom Brown League.

Trusting that God and his blessed Son shall watch over you and yours, and that he may spare and give you and your co-workers strength to carry out your plans, is the sincere wish of one of your boys.

I am sincerely and always will be,

Jack Murphy, No. 32177.

With some difficulty I persuaded my loyal partner to forego the name of Tom Brown in connection with the League. Before my departure for Europe, just a month after the day of my release, Jack was able to report a very satisfactory interview with Superintendent Riley, who had granted permission to start the League. Warden Rattigan's approval had been already secured.

During my six weeks' absence there was much talk on the subject, so far as it was possible for the prisoners to talk; and many kites passed back and forth among those most interested.

After my return events moved quickly, and on December 26 a free election was held in the different shops of the prison, to choose a committee of forty-nine to determine the exact nature and organization of the League, the general idea of which had been unanimously approved by show of hands at the conclusion of the chapel services on the Sunday previous.

Much interest was taken in the election, and there were some very close contests.

Three days after the election the members of the committee of forty-nine were brought to the chapel, and the meeting called to order by the Warden. By unanimous vote Thomas Brown, No. 33,333x, was made chairman; and then the Warden and the keepers retired. For the first time in the history of Auburn Prison a body of convicts were permitted a full and free discussion of their own affairs. The discussion was not only free but most interesting, as the committee contained men of all kinds, sentenced for all sorts of offenses—first, second and third termers.

This is not the place to go into details concerning the Mutual Welfare League of Auburn Prison; that is another story. It is enough to say that the by-laws of the League were carefully formulated by a subcommittee of twelve; and after full discussion in the committee of forty-nine were reported by that committee to the whole body of prisoners on January 11 and unanimously adopted. On February 12 the first meeting of the League was held.

Let me try to describe it.

It is the afternoon of Lincoln's Birthday. Once again I am standing on the stage of the assembly room of Auburn Prison, but how different is the scene before me. Busy and willing hands have transformed the dreary old place. The stage has been made into a real stage—properly boxed and curtained; the posts through the room are wreathed with colored papers; trophies and shields fill the wall spaces; the front of the gallery is gaily decorated. Everywhere are green and white, the colors of the League, symbolic of hope and truth. Painted on the curtain is a large shield with the monogram of the League and its motto, suggested by one of the prisoners, "Do good. Make good." At the back of the stage over the national flag a portrait of Lincoln smiles upon this celebration of a new emancipation.

At about quarter past two the tramp of men is heard and up the stairs and through the door come marching nearly 1,400 men (for all but seventeen of the prisoners have joined the League). Each man stands proudly erect and on his breast appears the green and white button of the League, sign and symbol of a new order of things. At the side of the companies march the assistant sergeants-at-arms and the members of the Board of Delegates—the governing body of the League; and on the coat of each is displayed a small green and white shield—his badge of authority.

No such perfect discipline has ever been seen before in Auburn Prison, and yet there is not a guard or keeper present except the new P. K. or Deputy Warden, who in an unofficial capacity stands near the door, watching to see how this miracle is being worked. In the usual place of the P. K. stands one of the prisoners, the newly-elected Sergeant-at-Arms, whose keen eye and forceful, quiet manner stamp him as a real leader of men.

In perfect order company after company marches in, and as soon as seated the men join in the general buzz of conversation, like any other human beings assembled for an entertainment. There is no disorder, nothing but natural life and animation.

I look out over the audience—and my mind turns back to the day before I entered prison, when I spoke to the men from this stage. What is it that has happened? What transformation has taken place? It suddenly occurs to me that this audience is no longer gray; why did I ever think it so? "Gray and faded and prematurely old," I had written of that rigid audience—each man sitting dull and silent under the eye of his watchful keeper, staring straight ahead, not daring to turn his head or to whisper.

Now there are no keepers, and each man is sitting easily and naturally, laughing and chatting with his neighbor. There is color in the faces and life in the eyes. I had never noticed before the large number of fine-looking young men. I can hardly believe it is the same gray audience I spoke to less than five short months ago. What does it all mean?

For this first meeting, the Executive Committee of the League has planned a violin and piano recital. For two hours the men listen attentively and with many manifestations of pleasure to good music by various composers varying from Bach and Beethoven to Sullivan and Johann Strauss.

170

Between the first and second parts of the programme, we have an encouraging report from the Secretary of the League, none other than our friend Richards, whose cynical pessimism of last July has been replaced by an almost flamboyant optimism as he toils night and day in the service of the League. We have also speeches of congratulation and good cheer from two other members of the Commission on Prison Reform, who have come from a distance to greet this dawn of the new era.

Then after the applause for the last musical number has died away, the long line of march begins again. In perfect order and without a whisper after they have fallen into line, the 1,400 men march back and shut themselves into their cells. One of the prison keepers who stands by, watching this wonderful exhibition of discipline, exclaims in profane amazement, "Why in Hell can't they do that for us?"

Why indeed?

The men have been back in their cells about an hour when an unexpected test is made of their loyalty and self-restraint. As I am about to leave the prison and stand chatting with Richards at his desk in the back office, the electric lights begin to flicker and die down.

Richards and I have just been talking of the great success of the League's first meeting and the good conduct of the men. "Now you will have the other side of it," says Richards. "Listen and you will hear the shouts and disorder that always come when the lights go out."

Dimmer and dimmer grow the lights, while Richards and I listen intently at the window in the great iron door which opens onto the gallery of the north wing.

Not a sound.

The lights go entirely out, and still not a sound. Not even a cough comes from the cells to disturb the perfect silence.

We remain about half a minute in the dark, listening at the door. Then the lights begin to show color, waver, grow lighter, go out altogether for a second, and then burn with a steady brightness.

I look at Richards. He is paler than usual, but there is a bright gleam in his eyes. "I would not have believed it possible," he says impressively, "such a thing has never happened in this prison before. The men always yell when the lights go out. In all my experience I have never known anything equal to that. I don't understand it.

"If anyone had told me the League could do such a thing," he

171

continues, "I would have laughed at them. Yet there it is. I have no further doubts now about our success."

As I leave the prison again, there ring in my ears the questions: What has happened? What does it all mean?

It means just one thing—my friend—for it is you now, you individually, to whom I am speaking; it means that these prisoners are men—real men—your brethren—and mine.

It means that as they are men they should be treated like men.

It means that if you treat them like beasts it will be hard for them to keep from degenerating into beasts. If you treat them like men you can help them to rise.

It means that if you trust them they will show themselves worthy of trust.

It means that if you place responsibility upon them they will rise to it.

Perhaps some may think that I am leaving out of consideration the direct religious appeal that can be made to the prisoners. By no means. I have no intention of underrating the religious appeal. Under the old depressing conditions it is about the only appeal that can be made. But the religious appeal, to be really effective, must be based upon a treatment of the prisoner somewhat in accordance with the precepts of religion. Preaching a religion of brotherly love to convicts while you are treating them upon a basis of diabolical hatred is a discouraging performance.

Give the prisoner fair treatment; discard your System based upon revenge; build up a new System based upon a temporary exile of the offender from Society until he can show himself worthy to be granted a new opportunity; and then give him a chance to build up his character while in retirement by free exercise of the faculties necessary for wise discrimination and right choice of action. Then your religious appeal to the prisoner will not be flagrantly contradicted by every sight and sound about him.

In one of the prisons in a neighboring state, I saw hanging up in the bare, unsightly room they called a chapel, a large illuminated text: Love One Another.

It seemed to me I had never before encountered such terrible, bitter, humiliating sarcasm.

At first sight it seems almost a miracle—the change that is being wrought under Superintendent Riley and Warden Rattigan in Auburn Prison. But in truth there is nothing really extraordinary about it—it is no miracle; unless it be a miracle to discard error and to replace it by truth. The results of a practical application of faith and hope and love often seem miraculous, but as a matter of fact such results are as logical as any geometrical demonstration.

When a man, treated like a beast, snarls and bites you say, "This is the conduct of an abnormal creature—a criminal." When a prisoner, treated like a man, nobly responds you cry, "A miracle!"

What folly! Both these things are as natural as two and two making four.

The real miracle is when men who have been treated for many years like beasts persist in retaining their manhood.

A prisoner is kept for half a generation in conditions so terrible and degrading that the real wonder is how he has kept his sanity, and then he asks only for a chance to show where Society has made a mistake, begs only for an opportunity to be of service to his brethren.

Donald Lowrie and Ed Morrell, laying aside their own wrongs and making light of their own sufferings, as they arouse not only the state of California but the whole nation to a sense of responsibility for the shocking conditions in our prisons; Jack Murphy, turning his back upon the chance of a pardon, asking nothing for himself, seeking only how he can do the most good to his fellow-prisoners; these are the real miracles; when the spirit of God thus works in the hearts of men.

I have talked with no sensible person who proposes to sentimentalize over the law-breaker. Call the prison by any name you please, yet prisons of some sort we must have so long as men commit crime; and that from present indications will be for many generations to come. So far from setting men free from prison you and I, sensible people as I trust we are, would, if we could have our own way, put more men in prison than are there now; for we should send up all who now escape by the wiles of crooked lawyers, and we should include the crooked lawyers. But behind the prison walls we should relax the iron discipline—the hideous, degrading, unsuccessful system of silence and punishment—and substitute a system fair to all men, a limited freedom, and work in the open air.

A new penology is growing up to take the place of the old. The Honor System is being tried in many states and, to the surprise of the old expert, is found practicable. But at Auburn Prison an experiment is in progress that goes straight to the very heart of the Problem. In the minds of many the reform of the Prison System has been accomplished when a cold-hearted, brutal autocrat has been replaced by a kindly, benevolent autocrat. But so far as the ultimate success of the prisoner is concerned there is not much to choose. The former says, "Do this, or I will punish you." The latter says, "Do this, and I will reward you." Both leave altogether out of sight the fact that when the man leaves the shelter of the prison walls there will be no one either to threaten punishment or offer reward. Unless he has learned to do right on his own initiative there is no security against his return to prison.

"Do you know how men feel when they leave such a place as this?" said one of the Auburn third-termers to me, during the League discussions. "Well, I'll tell you how I felt when I had finished my first term. I just hated everybody and everything; and I made up my mind that I'd get even."

There spoke the spirit of the old System.

During the same discussion another member of the committee, an Italian, had been listening with the most careful attention to all that had been said and particularly to the assertions that when responsibility was assumed by the prisoners at their League meetings there must be no fights or disorder. Then when someone else had said, "The men must leave their grudges behind when they come to the meetings of the League," Tony stood on his feet to give more effect to his words and spoke to this effect:

"Yes, Mr. Chairman, the men must leave their grudges behind. Let me tell you some thing.

"Two months ago at Sing Sing I did have a quarrel with my friend, and this is what he did to me"; and the speaker pointed to a large scar which disfigures his left cheek. His "friend," when Tony was lying asleep in the hospital, had taken a razor and slit his mouth back to the cheekbone.

A hard glint of light came into Tony's eyes as he said, "And I have been waiting for my revenge ever since. And he is here—here in this prison."

Then the light in the eyes softened and the hard look on the face relaxed as Tony added, slowly and impressively, "But now I see, Mr. Chairman, that I can not have my revenge without doing a great wrong to fourteen hundred other men.

"So I give it up. He can go."

There spoke the prison spirit of the future.

THE END

174